Passages of a Stream

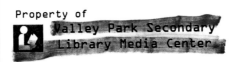

Passages of a Stream
A Chronicle of the Meramec

James P. Jackson

University of Missouri Press
Columbia, 1984

Copyright © 1984 by
The Curators of the University of Missouri
University of Missouri Press, Columbia, Missouri 65211
Library of Congress Catalog Card Number
Printed and bound in the United States of America

Library of Congress Cataloging in Publication Data

Jackson, James P.
    Passages of a stream.

    1. Stream ecology—Missouri—Meramec River.
2. Meramec River (Mo.)   I. Title.
QH105.M8J33   1983   508.778'6   83–16752
ISBN 0–8262–0418–X

Photographs are by the author except for the following:

by Don Wooldridge, courtesy Missouri Department of
    Conservation, 29;
courtesy the James Foundation, St. James, Mo., 51, 53;
by Charles Phelps Cushing, courtesy Margaret J. Camp-
    bell, 60, 62;
by Al Foster, courtesy St. Louis County Department of
    Parks and Recreation, 73;
courtesy St. Louis County Department of Parks and
    Recreation, 74, 128, 129, 132, 135;
by James Vandike, courtesy Missouri Department of
    Natural Resources, 95.

To all who worked successfully to preserve
the Meramec as a free-flowing stream

Preface

A deer leaps up from a gravelbar to a high mud bank, appearing larger than life in the mist of early morning. A concert of birdsong fills the green corridor of the stream; it is punctuated by the splash of a smallmouth bass and the staccato of a pileated woodpecker drumming on a sycamore. The humid air is slightly scented with willows. I hold my canoe paddle gently and work it slowly, avoiding the kind of bold and noisy strokes that might shatter a reverie.

Soon the sun is rising above wooded hills to clear away the mist. A slight breeze ripples across my bow and chases warm updrafts; they send vultures circling over a high, rocky bluff. Look alive, Jackson. The approach of a sparkling riffle now catches my attention; although it is a minor challenge, if I get careless it could send me crashing into the bank or up on a snag, tipping me over. But I slip through easily and the next pool is another revelation, a clearing of cobwebs from the brain, an awakening to the beauty that is all around. That's the way it is on a perfect morning on a lovely stream.

The stream I describe is totally unrestrained, undammed, and free flowing. It is the Meramec of the Ozarks. For anyone to argue that it is just another small river would be as ridiculous as claiming that all people are alike. Every stream is different; each is a unique, living entity. I refer to the Meramec as a *stream* because I see important differences between rivers and streams, and for most of its length, the Meramec does not fit my definition of a river. Sizable enough to gather riches from numerous tributaries, a river is really too big for intimacy. Its values in today's scheme of things are too impersonal, no longer adapted to such simple pleasures as canoeing, swimming, or pole and line fishing. It is more apt to serve barge traffic, and its valley embraces such things as urban sprawl, highways, railroads, air terminals, and industrial parks. Its voluminous flow conveniently tends to dilute any pollutants dumped into it and sends them quickly to sea, along with wasted soil. Civilization crowds the banks of a river, fights natural floods with levees and, not too success-fully, with high dams that serve as monuments to engineering skill and human industry. And civilization forever marches up the valley to threaten the headwaters—the real streams. A river commands respect but seldom personal devotion; the valley is too broad, the hills too distant, the water too dirty.

A stream is the appealing child of a river. While it may at times have fits of unruly flooding, it normally flows with the grace and clarity of youthfulness. It gladly offers gifts to what-ever world awaits downstream, but it also tends to harbor a closely knit community of life within its small valley. Unlike the river it flows or grows into, a stream is not simply an ag-gregate of separate entities that have joined into conformity. It has distinctive features that are direct reflections of the im-mediate surroundings. Whether we dare to admit it or not, a stream such as the Meramec has no peer. Any threat to its integrity by such forces as creeping blight or dam builders is, in effect, a violation of something irreplaceable. We have plenty of rivers, but true streams are getting scarce.

The name *Meramec* is of obscure Indian origin, and various translations relate it to springs of one description or another; one claim, however, is that it means "catfish stream." The Meramec originates in heavily wooded Ozark hills, flows en-tirely in Missouri, and ends in the Mississippi just below St. Louis. Its upper portions exert great attraction for recreation seekers from the metropolitan area and beyond. None of it is wilderness, but when summer's green shades are drawn out along wooded banks, the scenery can be pleasing even to a purist. And it changes with every meander; there are steep hills, high bluffs, caves, springs, and abundant wildlife. Ex-cept when in flood, it offers clean gravelbars for overnight camping. But then it approaches St. Louis.

The lower Meramec valley is crowded with industry, high-ways, shopping centers, and nearly a thousand stilt-legged, dilapidated old clubhouses strung out along the banks. In some places gravel diggings torture the channel, and in others the banks have become nothing more than unsanitary land-fills. While visions of the natural stream fade upriver with time and progress, the specter of environmental sickness follows close behind.

Yet this is the stream and the river I know best, and what has really brought me to write about it can perhaps best be described as a childhood love affair. As a city boy I was sent by my father to spend two delightful weeks at a summer camp on the right bank of the Meramec. Happily I worked my way into spending all of the next three summers there as a non-paid employee, doing such chores as cleaning the mess hall tables, sweeping the camp office, and running errands. In my free time, which was generously granted, I learned to paddle a canvas-covered canoe, try my luck as a fisherman, swing from a grapevine into the swimming hole, follow the flight of handsome wood ducks around the bend, and thrill to nocturnal serenades by frogs and barred owls and whippoorwills from numerous gravelbar campsites. Such long-remembered impressions are the bonds of my enduring love affair with the Meramec. Each return to it becomes a sort of baptism; it washes away the sins of too much civilized living and renews my faith in the natural world that is so terribly endangered by the industry of men.

I consider nothing unusual about this love affair, how it started or how it has been kept alive. Judging from concerns that have been widely generated by problems of the Meramec, many others must share my feelings. There has been the urban blight that began creeping up the valley before my time, then the final threat of a dam to be built by the U.S. Army Corps of Engineers on the still-lovely upper portion. But many people obviously shared my devotion—so many, in fact, that they halted an almost irreversible process, teaming up against a bureaucratic entrenchment that thrives on the pork barrel of great public works projects. And they beat the dam.

This book is my tribute to all free-flowing streams. The writing of it has led me into Ozark hills, backward into ancient origins, into the political fray over the dam, and down the lovely vistas that seem to attract more canoeists with every passing year. I hope that my pilgrimage can be enjoyed by others.

*   *   *

In the writing of this book I am indebted to the following persons who read selected portions of a preliminary draft: Bruce Stinchcomb (paleontology); Jerry Vineyard (caves and springs); Carl Chapman (archeology); Milton Rafferty (Ozark geography and history); Ford Hughes (Maramec Iron Works); George Fleener (recreation seekers); Jerry Sugerman (the dam controversy). After the helpful criticism from these knowledgeable people, any errors relative to the parenthesized topics must be mine.

A number of biologists with the Missouri Department of Conservation also advised me on various forms of wildlife: Alan Buchanan (mussels); Richard Clawson and James Gardner (cave biology); David Erickson (muskrats); David Graber (wood ducks); Willian Pflieger (smallmouth bass); Linden Trial (insects). Other staff members of the Missouri Department of Conservation who advised or helped me in significant ways include Joseph Bachant, Bill Crawford, Mac Johnson, Jim Keefe, and James Whitley.

To complete the list of persons to whom I am indebted for supplying relevant information, I include Francis Bruno, Carol Springer Curtis, Joseph Cushing, Jim DePardo, Hal Donnelly, Walter Eschbach, Catherine French, Richard Gaffney, Ben Knox, Vance Lischer, Delbert Moutray, Don Rimbach, Eileen Sherrill, and Judy Woltjen. Thanks to all.

J. P. J.
Marthasville, Mo.
June 1983

Contents

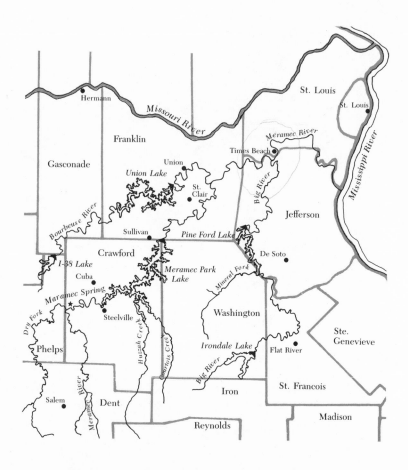

▲   Sites of proposed dams on the Meramec and its major tributaries;
U.S. Army Corps of Engineers, Meramec Basin Project, 1971

★   Maramec Spring

1   Beginnings

To pinpoint the exact source of the Meramec would be as difficult as locating the first drop to touch ground from a summer rainstorm. Establishing its origin in time would be equally trying. Both, however, are worth searching for; there is much to learn about a stream from its beginnings.

Every drop that falls along the north-sloping edge of a certain wooded Ozark ridge, every trickle of winter snowmelt, may be considered a source in itself. Each one absorbs a few molecules of mineral nutrient as it gravitates over or seeps into the rocky terrain. Each one shares in a miniscule joining of enrichment—a sort of protoplasm of the Meramec—and contributes to its real birth. Depending on the viewpoint, a stream has a billion embryonic beginnings or it has just a few.

In extreme closeup the source is raindrops and trickles of snowmelt; from a broader perspective it is a meeting of gravel-filled ravines into which all but the heaviest rainfall quickly disappears. Porosity is an important feature of the entire watershed. There are cracks in the foundation bedrock, seeps finding their way through it, hidden caves whose only surface clues are sinkholes plugged with mud and sometimes holding water. Except after prolonged downpours, there is no surface flow for the first few miles. The Meramec really starts where two semidry branches meet in a small valley, southeast of Salem, in Dent County.

From birth the Meramec is cradled in thin, gravelly soil that overlays porous beds of sedimentary rock deposited by ancient seas. It is swaddled in oak, hickory, and other deciduous trees, with scattered groves of cedars on the ridges above. It is watched over by deer, raccoons, squirrels, wild turkeys, hawks, and other creatures too numerous to mention. Its infant flow, at first a channel narrow enough for a boy to jump across, is nursed by small springs and grows with each new source joining it, through a continuing series of clear pools and lively riffles. The Meramec in its upper reaches

1

A winter scene at Shaw Arboretum, in Franklin County.

ebbs and flows with the seasons and the years, gathering whatever nourishment it can from the hills; this is the way of all streams.

The Ozark land through which it flows, while in places steeply pitched by erosion, is not the mountainous terrain of awesome canyons and snow-capped peaks. It was not shaped by volcanoes or violent upheavals. It is a broad plateau with convoluted ridges, deeply wrinkled with ravines and small valleys.

Here is a stream that shows no inclination to race headlong in pursuit of its destiny. It is not urged downward by the precipitous slopes of high peaks, just hills. If the Meramec were to follow the straightest possible course, it would travel only eighty miles from source to Mississippi. But, thank goodness, it graces the landscape with countless bends and meanders for three times that distance, first in a northward direction, then generally eastward. Near the start it is fairly straight, a mere infant with neither the volume nor the erosive strength to cut bends into bedrock. But later it must drop eight hundred feet to reach the Mississippi, and so, after some twenty miles, it begins carving a series of barely perceptible steps.

Each step is a riffle around a gravelbar, many of which are located at sharp bends and confronted by rocky bluffs that tell how the Meramec has shaped its valley—carved it with gravel and silt-laden water as the principal tool. The riffles alternate with gently curving stretches of placid water, interludes between bursts of creative energy. Sharpening meanders and bigger bluffs tell the downstream story of its work. Some of the bends become U-shaped and the bluffs heighten from 20 feet to spectacular rock faces 150 feet high, near the site of a dam intended to impound the entire valley.

Near the upper end of what would have become Meramec Park Lake, the main stream is joined by the first two of four sizable tributaries, the beautifully clear Huzzah and Courtois (pronounced Code-away by natives), which run parallel for some distance before merging into the Meramec from the right. At this junction all three are similar enough to reinforce each other as true Ozark streams. The third and fourth tributaries, however, are quite different. From the left is the Bourbeuse, skirting the northern edge of the basin; there it has carved a channel in softer rock, much of it sandstone, and carrying more silt than gravel, it is somewhat sluggish when compared with the first two and much more meandering. The last major tributary, from the right, has the exaggerated name of Big River, and it borders the eastern edge of the Ozark Plateau, where it originates in ancient hills of granite. Each of these four arteries, like the Meramec itself, is unique; together they serve to diversify and enrich the broadening valley into which they flow.

Every stream system matures as it travels and gathers from its watershed, but it also develops through time; it did not originate in a year, nor in a century, nor even in a millennium. The Meramec happens to be a very old stream, and its journey through time is not easy to follow. Nevertheless, to un-

Bluff and bar on the upper Meramec.

derstand its present we must fathom something of its origin. As with any living entity, it is a product of both the present environment and inheritance from the past.

The ancient, primordial source was the sea, which created sedimentary rock that cradles the Meramec for nearly all its length. The process began during a period known as the Ordovician, named after a site in Wales, where typical fossils of the period were first studied. The Ordovician period occurred roughly 500 million years ago. During that time, and for varying intervals thereafter, what is now the Ozark Plateau was in reality a warm, shallow sea that lapped at the edge of a young continent. Fine muds and coarser sands were continually being washed into this basin from a totally barren landscape, before the green mantle of life had come ashore to anchor it against unrelenting erosion.

For many millions of years the sediments accumulated, thickened, reacted with dissolved minerals in the huge evaporating dish of a warm and shallow sea. The chemistry that took place, today veiled by the immensity of time, was what made possible the rock foundations of the Meramec as we know them.

A superabundance of magnesium, common to all sea water, combined with calcium carbonate sediments to create massive beds of the compound calcium magnesium carbonate; with pressure and time these beds solidified into the white rock dolomite. Blobs of jellylike silicon dioxide, meanwhile, became trapped within; they compressed into layers of extremely hard chert, the kind of material eventually used by Indians to make spear and arrow points. Interspersed in places were beachlike deposits that became sandstone. The scenic bluffs of today's Meramec are mostly dolomite. Gravelbars below them also exhibit fragments of this rock, but because it is softer and more vulnerable to dissolving action by water, the bars tend to show a higher percentage of chert than originally existed.

Within both the dolomite and chert, wherever they appear,

cryptic pages of fossil history may sometimes by viewed, because life was then quite abundant in the sea. Primitive animals ingested a living soup of green algae that manufactured food in the sunlit shallows. Some creatures had already evidenced biological progress by eating each other, and all yielded their remains, at least the indelible portions, to a graveyard of accumulating deposits. Their record may be found in exposed bluffs, in caves, and in fragments of rock on practically any gravelbar of the Meramec.

The softer parts of living things seldom preserve well as fossils; only the hard parts tend to leave clear imprints. But certain primitive algae that absorbed silica as part of their life activities did leave clues to their existence long ago. They have been discovered along the Meramec as spheres of concentric chert leaves known as cryptozoons, yet more aptly described as petrified cabbages. They are usually found in groups, and paleontologists believe that their abundance in the ancient, shallow seas caused them to form extensive reefs, somewhat like corals of today.

Also to be found along the Meramec are fossils of early snails and other mollusks. One group, ancestors of today's exquisite chambered nautilus, had the internal partitions but showed only a hint of coiling. Some of these creatures were shaped like cowhorns, were among the largest of their time, and possessed eyes, allowing them to be among the first predators to exist. Sharing this role of underwater hunters were the smaller trilobites. These long-extinct relatives of modern crustaceans evolved so many structural variations that their fossils can be used as indicators of relative age for the rocks in which they appear. Each span of time, each sedimentary deposit, supported its own array of trilobite species. As a graveyard of terribly old fossils, the Meramec rock strata also harbor evidence of other strange creatures: cone-shaped monoplacophorans, which scavenged on the bottom; clamlike brachiopods, each armed with a pair of hooked tentacles; stems of crinoids, which must have looked more like plants than animals. There was a wealth of life, and much of it contributed, by its remains, to the rock that today pleases the eye as scenic bluffs.

The entire plateau that underlies the Meramec is of sedimentary rock. Fossils suggest how long ago the material was deposited; they do not, however, tell anything about how the Ozark region was lifted above sea level. The earth is, and always has been, a more or less flexible sphere with a relatively thin crust floating on a core of denser, molten material. Over long stretches of time, certain portions have been pushed under, thus allowing other parts to bulge up in response—but always on a massive, incomprehensible scale. Just how such forces might have lifted the Ozark Plateau is not clear, but there is plenty of evidence that it happened a number of times.

Geologists believe that the entire Ozark region was alternately elevated and submerged. Every exposure above sea level brought erosion and the wearing away of some rock; every inundation allowed more sediments to be laid down. Each separate stratum, known as a formation and given a place name, can be identified by its precise chemical composition and the fossils it contains. There are many such strata, each one serving as a page in an extremely thick book whose chapters can be delineated by major geologic time periods.

But part of reading the rocks involves acknowledging that certain pages and even major chapters are missing regionally. Wherever this happens, circumstantial evidence points to erosion as having been the culprit. In other words, lack of an expected formation and its diagnostic fossils does not mean the page was never written; it merely tells us that a stratum of rock was removed—ripped off by forces of water or wind wearing it away. Then after erosion came another inundation by the sea and the deposition of more material, always on top. This process happened repeatedly in the Ozark region, leaving between strata dividing lines often visible to a geologist.

All major chapters of geologic time written after the Ordovician period are gone from the Ozark region except around its rim. There they are represented by a fringe of rock outcrops close to the Mississippi River, flanking the lowest por-

tion of the Meramec. The outcrops tell us that local chapters
were indeed written but later eroded from the main portion
of the plateau. Gone from most of the Meramec's watershed is
any evidence of steaming fern forest that probably existed
there some 300 million years ago, of mighty dinosaurs that
may have roamed there 100 million years ago, or of the early
birds and mammals that succeeded them.

What all of this tells us is that a truly mountainous uplifting
must have occurred to initiate such a thorough scalping of the
Ozark region, right down to Ordovician rock in most places.
The Meramec in its geologic beginnings surely played an important role in the erosional process. Much of this portion of
the stream's story is to be discovered by exploring its many
caves.

2   Etchings of Time

The Meramec harbors many secrets. If it were tumbling out of newly uplifted mountains, just beginning to carve an original channel, this would not be the case. But the Ozark Plateau was repeatedly worn down and uplifted. Its headwaters may be outwardly youthful, but in terms of geologic time the Meramec is a stream that has experienced a long history of devious passages. We need to explore beneath the land's surface, to look beyond the obvious, to read this story.

The rock bluffs and steep-sided, meandering valley of the Meramec represent the top of a great spongeworks. Underground passages are in places both deeper and broader than the visible signs of erosion above. In the entire basin are at least two hundred known caves of various sizes; the exact count increases as new ones are found practically every year. In addition, both in the valley and hills bordering the Meramec and its tributaries, there are caves completely hidden, with no openings to the surface. Well drillers become aware of them, though vaguely, whenever their diamond-impregnated bits slide through mud pockets in thick beds of hard, dolomitic limestone. These diagnostic soft spots vary in depth from a few to many feet and are evidence of ancient cavities long ago packed with finely sifted mud that somehow entered from an eroded landscape above. Drillers who penetrate such cavities cannot begin to guess how far they extend in any horizontal direction, but new ones are breached nearly every time a well is sunk into the watershed. Exploration and study of caves and springs can reveal the story of how water could have etched into the watershed a sort of subterranean Swiss cheese.

There are a number of sites in the Meramec basin that tell this story, but a good place to begin is in either one of its two largest caves, both of which are commercially well known. Advertising that attests to the wonders of Meramec Caverns is plastered on barn roofs and billboards along many midwestern highways; some of it boasts that it was once a hideout for Jesse James and his outlaw gang. Onondaga Cave is now part of a state park by the same name, and its late owner—the man who commercialized both of them—claimed that it was discovered by Daniel Boone. While there is doubt that the notorious James or the legendary Boone ever visited either place, nobody can prove otherwise. These two magnificent caves, twenty-six miles apart by water, are both adjacent to the left bank. Meramec Caverns is below the spot where the Corps of Engineers was to dam the stream; Onondaga, a bit smaller but widely recognized as one of the loveliest in America, is above the dam site. Most of it would have been permanently flooded by the lake project.

If we were to join a group visiting Meramec Caverns, we would be assigned a guide selected for the job on the basis of his ability to spiel off a blending of fact and folklore, invariably with an Ozark twang. As he leads us through dripping, winding passages and large chambers on concreted walks, he flips on and off colored lights to produce eerie shadows and lend dramatic hues to the exquisite natural formations. He points out imaginary figures in silhouette and gives them colorful names. He tells how Art Linkletter and Lassie once brought television fame to the Caverns and how its vast chambers qualify as official nuclear bomb shelters; tourists are impressed. For benefit of those who might be offended by the garishness of multicolored lights, he stops to announce that he is about to show off the Caverns in all the true splendor of natural lighting. Then he flips off the lights and waits for his charges to giggle in absolute darkness. We don't learn much from all this but can certainly admit to being entertained.

If we ask him the age of Meramec Caverns, he's likely to give a quick, parroted answer in the range of a million years—a good rounded figure. If he is at all knowledgeable, he may correctly explain that caves originate from what is known simply as the solution process. Water, falling as rain or snow, picks up small amounts of carbon dioxide from the air and humic acid from decomposing humus in the soil surface. A weak solution of carbonic acid is produced, capable of slowly etching, or dissolving, the vulnerable dolomitic limestone that underlies the Meramec and surrounding hills. Over great spans of time, then, the dissolving action creates caves and springs.

As the guide speaks, we are mesmerized by the strange environment, by the echoing of his voice, the silent passing of bats, and the constant dripping of water from the tips of hanging stalactites, down upon the tips of upright stalagmites or glistening over the marbled surface of an exquisite rock drapery. We wonder how such a tedious process has anything to do with the forming of cave chambers as huge as athletic arenas. It doesn't. Probing our own chilled imaginations, we try somehow to compare cave making to whatever process carved out something like the Grand Canyon. We cannot.

The Grand Canyon is a product of scouring action by water carrying a load of rock particles while moving on a steep gradient over surfaces vulnerable to freezing and thawing by changeable weather. The process is one of abrasion by a sort of liquid sandpaper, and various types of rock differ in their resistance to it. Upper strata of sandstone and limestone, for instance, are more easily eroded than the granites below them, but all of them wear down faster than cave rock being etched by weak acid. The Grand Canyon, although nearly a mile deep, is estimated to be less than ten million years old. The much smaller Meramec Caverns, in spite of whatever age is parroted by a guide, is probably much older.

Cave making involves some scouring, or erosion, especially in the later stages; yet the etching is far more significant. The constant dripping that mesmerizes us, except when it chills our ears, nose, or neck, plays no part whatsoever in the process. What we admire as lovely formations of dripstone and flowstone do not represent cave expansion; they indicate a filling of space, or cave senility. The deposits grow as a result of carbon dioxide being released into the cave atmosphere by water seeping in from above; this in turn reduces the water's mild acidity and crystallizes previously dissolved minerals. The formations grow, ever so slowly, eventually to fill the passages and chambers along with accumulated mud. Then the cave dies and is buried, in a process that seems to reverse its ancient creation.

As we follow our guide through cloistered and winding passageways, we come to notice a small underground stream entrenched in heavy, sticky mud below the level of our cemented walkway. A similar but larger watercourse is one of the first things we would notice in Onondaga. We can rightly assume, even though the flow is now quite small, that once it was greater and that it carved its present twisting channel even as the Meramec carved its valley with the aid of abrasive mud. Now we might try to imagine how gravity helped the stream to create a system of large chambers by constantly etching and eroding downward while air-filled spaces expanded above. But here again it is easy to misinterpret the visible clues. The underground stream did somewhat deepen its channel, but only after the cave was already formed, almost as though to deceive us. The truth is, Meramec Caverns, Onondaga, and all others within the region developed as completely water-filled tubes. They began and grew as springs. To visualize what really happened, we need to explore the largest spring that joins the Meramec along its entire course.

The cold, clear water of Maramec Spring (the different spelling is not an error) gushes out from beneath the cool shade of a north-facing bluff. A hundred yards downstream is a series of holding pools for trout and a low dam, beyond which is a half-mile-long spring branch, well stocked with rainbow trout. The average volume of the spring is nearly a hundred million gallons per day, enough to supply the usual needs of all the people living in Kansas City. It emerges in visible swirls—some describe it as a cold boil—due to a narrow constriction in the exit. Internally, the tube from which water emerges beneath the bluff, becomes progressively larger. The expanding of the tube was discovered by scuba divers who once penetrated the spring for more than a quarter of a mile. With powerful battery-operated lights and air tanks strapped to their backs, they pulled themselves against the strong emerging current with handholds on jagged rock faces, down beyond the constriction and into an expanded chamber where the current was gentle, down 190 feet below the level of the exit. The only factors that kept them from going farther were their own limitations and those of their equipment; the inky blackness seemed to go on endlessly. Nowhere did they find a single air pocket. The system was completely water filled, and similar explorations in other large Ozark springs have told the same story.

The volume of this spring is both large and never failing, but where does it come from? A partial answer may be found in the wooded, hardscrabble hills fanning southward from the exit. There a hiker would notice scattered sinkholes, funnel-shaped pits in the terrain where water tends to vanish as it does through the open drain of a tub. Residents of the area observe that certain local creeks flow only during spells of prolonged, heavy rainfall; normally they are dry gravelbeds. Obviously, the rockbound hills are porous and riddled with passages. Yet this does not fully explain just how extensive the spongeworks must be in order to sustain the spring at all times, even in the driest season of the driest year.

Measured discharge of the spring does vary considerably with local precipitation. Hydrologists have recorded a definite relationship between seasonal fluctuations and the lowest (base) level of water in domestic wells within seven miles of the spring. Also, by taking into account the region's average annual precipitation and carefully monitoring surface runoff from local drainages, they have calculated that the contributing area must include at least 150 square miles. The source of all this water is believed to be a broad dome of water-filled rock strata whose vertical dimensions extend both above and well below the valley of the Meramec. It must be so to generate the necessary pressure for bringing a cold boil upward at least 190 feet.

Maramec Spring can be viewed as a working model to show how most—and possibly all—Ozark caves have developed as totally water-filled tubes. Meramec Caverns, meanwhile, demonstrates how a cave begins to refill and, ultimately, to die. But all this still does not tell us what changes take place in the unimaginable span between these two stages.

When the hills were pushed up from the sea in the dim geological past, however gently, the sedimentary strata surely must have suffered cracks and faults from various stresses. It was then that the etching agent of weak carbonic acid must have begun seeping into vulnerable dolomite, downward in cracks and horizontally between bedding planes, or layers of deposit. Surface erosion of the elevated landscape also began scratching out rivulets and merging them into the primordial Meramec. But always, wherever water penetrated the rock strata, it sought its own level. Below the valley floor—especially below it—water pushed laterally in all directions, through any means possible, by hydrostatic pressure from the weight of whatever volume was sealed in the hills directly above. And when the Meramec cut its channel downward to intersect underground passages, it caused leaks to develop. The hills were porous reservoirs, valley springs became upturned faucets, and deeply hidden tubes served as plumbing to direct the flow. The rate of solution process, or actual tube enlargement, increased in direct proportion to the force and volume of water passing through. Caves were in the making.

Time is relative, and it often needs speeding up for us to visualize geologic events. If we could imagine ticking off centuries as we count seconds on a clock, then we might have seen a proliferating of springs as the primordial Meramec continued to deepen its valley from surface erosion. But such a lowering of the valley over a long span of time would also tend to drain water reservoirs in the hills above. This actually happened, and it is what brought on the eventual emptying of water-filled tubes, beginning with the highest.

During those long centuries, as accelerated by our imaginary clock, any extended period of drought served to increase the draining process; prolonged spells of heavy precipitation caused emerging caves to refill. Meanwhile, the deepest water-filled passages were receiving a certain amount of material from an eroding surface above, mostly in the form of finely sifted mud, washing in through sinkholes and cracks in cave ceilings. With adequate flow, this sediment was carried in suspension toward the nearest spring exit in the valley. But whenever upper passages were drained, thus reducing hydrostatic pressure below the level of the stream, deeper currents were slowed, allowing a settling of sediments. In other words, as upper passages became air filled, deeper spongeworks tended to become mud filled.

Finally, something else occurred geologically. It was an event that occurred over many thousands of years; since it happened so slowly, so gently, a more specific estimate is impossible. At any rate, the entire Ozark region experienced another one of its periodic upliftings. The Meramec and its valley reveal two hints of this uplift. First is the looping, meandering nature of today's Meramec and its valley. Second is the sizeable number of caves, now high and mostly empty, which long ago were formed as deep plumbing below the valley when it flowed at the level of today's hilltops.

To follow the sequence and place the hints in sharper focus, we go back to the primordial Meramec, with full reservoirs in the hills, deep plumbing beneath, and upturned faucets opened into the valley. Next, many centuries of surface erosion reduce the hills, lowering the reservoirs and reducing pressure below, gradually turning off the springs. The plumbing stagnates and fills with sediments. The Meramec, meanwhile, which originally sped downhill by the straightest possible course, slows to a lazy pace; it begins to meander, sluggishly, back and forth across an ever-widening valley. But once again the entire watershed is uplifted—not by the kind of violent upheaval that creates craggy mountains—but very slowly, imperceptibly. Finally there is the pull of gravity to speed up the stream's current, yet not so urgently as to make it straighten out; it cuts a deepening channel, but only within the boundaries of its previous meanders. This looping entrenchment of today's Meramec, an obvious clue to its rejuvenation, is also one of its most endearing qualities. It stretches out the scenery for its admirers; it extends the time by which a canoeist can enjoy drifting with the flow, from one curving vista into another.

The second clue to uplifting of the region, the many caves in the hills, indicates previously deep spongeworks that were stagnated and filled with sediments, then elevated. And now, wherever an underground drainage has cut through the packed mud and gravel, it has cleared their passages. The Meramec Caverns tour shows this as a small stream flowing within large air-filled chambers, collecting drops from lovely dripstone and flowstone formations plus whatever water enters from perforations in the ceiling. During periods of heavy rainfall it carries a burden of abrasive sediments and cuts the meandering channel below the cave floor, as though imitating the Meramec's behavior outside.

There is no simple way to decipher the precise history of each cave within the Meramec's watershed. Such an effort would be as unlikely as trying to pinpoint the age of a piece of dolomite on the basis of a single fossil fragment. It takes fossils of many kinds from a sedimentary rock layer to evaluate the ancient community of life and to measure its age accurately. A single cave formed in that same rock will not reveal all the secrets of cave origins. We can, however, make certain assumptions by taking a broad look at a whole community of caves. We can assume, for example, that the highest caves in the hills are the oldest, for they originated as deep plumbing systems during a cycle of erosion before the latest uplifting. In other words, they are older than the hills of today; they are older than the Grand Canyon.

We can also appreciate the fact that the processes go on, even today. They have left us a perfect model in Maramec Spring. The hills that feed into it have not been drained of their water table as is the case with Meramec Caverns, Onondaga, and many lesser cave systems. This tells us that while the Meramec is quite old, it is also very much alive in carving a destiny for its future.

3   Greening of the Hills

Water is surely the most pervasive force on earth. It works to level mountains. It carves hills, shapes valleys, creates lovely streams and rivers, leaches out springs and thus makes caves possible. It returns to the sea what it takes from the land, but repays the land by making possible the green mantle of life that has made our existence possible.

Life emerged from the primordial sea some time after the Ordovician period that created the Meramec's underpinnings. Until then the landscape was barren, totally dead. To visualize what happened we must again speed up the geologic clock to a rate that, even though totally unrealistic, is at least plausible. Life on land probably began with blobs of food-producing seaweed being washed ashore. Most of the green stuff died— was dried by wind and sun—but some of it survived, somehow, and found a means to establish a beachhead. It evolved some sort of primitive roots to entrench itself in preparation for invading the lowlands. It then inched away from the protective sea, advanced slowly, tediously, and after perhaps a hundred million years it was able to proliferate into vast, steaming forests of fernlike trees—the kind of vegetation that left us a legacy of coal deposits. Animals of course followed, all according to their own special patterns of evolution.

The Meramec was witness to none of this; it did not then exist. Although some life of the great Carboniferous age, or age of coal, did leave imprints on the Ozark Plateau that we see today, they can be found only around the rim. Indeed, the pages of that geological record have been for the most part removed; the sedimentary deposits that would have preserved them were uplifted and then eroded away. Besides, whatever plant life did grow along the Meramec when it first scratched a way across an elevated landscape was already advanced beyond the age of fern forests. By this time there had evolved new types of trees, primarily cone-bearing evergreens similar to the firs and pines of today. As succeeding generations of this upland forest lived and then died, the acid from decomposition of their needles and dead wood must surely have aided the solution process then beginning to create the Meramec's first springs and caves.

This earliest phase of the Meramec's history occurred some time after the extinction of great reptiles, such as dinosaurs, that once dominated the earth; that is, it occurred less than 75 million years ago. But to estimate that time more accurately is quite impossible, for this record too was eroded away. The Ozark Plateau was already wearing down to what it is now—mostly Ordovician rock of the original sea.

The Meramec had begun to establish a watershed, carving it into hills, shaping a valley, and starting to meander within it. The entire planet, meanwhile, was beginning to show its own peculiar signs of aging. It was no longer uniformly warm; there were times when certain portions of its surface felt the effect of gradual cooling. This climatic change, perhaps with other factors unimaginable to us, was causing ancient patterns of life either to evolve or to disappear.

Newly adapted plants and animals pushed older forms aside. The fern forests and great reptiles were now entombed in the geologic chronicle of fossilized remains. Even the cone-bearing trees were being challenged with new competition, though they would survive in many places to the present.

New trees evolved. They could drop their leaves in times of cold and their seeds were completely enclosed, unlike those of firs and pines. They were the deciduous trees that now dominate our temperate regions. Smaller plants devised an entirely different method for surviving in a changing climate; they retreated to their roots, letting their tops die during seasons of drought or extreme cold. They became our perennial herbs and grasses, and they along with the deciduous trees did a thorough job of clothing the landscape of the Meramec basin.

Animal life was also experiencing dramatic changes. Evolution had begun tinkering with certain small survivors of the reptilian age and had made them into flying reptiles. Soon it advanced these creatures and diversified them with ingenious adaptations into what are now among the most beautiful, graceful creatures on earth: modern birds. The earliest mammals, which apparently outwitted cumbersome reptilian types by remaining small and elusive, soon found the opportunity to expand their horizons. They along with the birds brought new life into the vacuum left by outclassed dinosaurs. Archaic mammals eventually grew into horses, camels, musk-oxen, bison, and piglike peccaries, all of which emerged upon the sunlit plains of the American continent. Tapirs, giant sloths, bears, wolves, saber-toothed tigers, and the predecessors of today's elephants roamed the woodlands along the Meramec. While its channel meandered gently in a maturing landscape and cave systems stagnated with mud beneath, the Meramec and its tributaries were supporting a community of ever-increasing diversity.

But then, 2 million years ago more or less, the Pleistocene epoch, the Ice Age, arrived. It was not the first time that a great, domed sheet of ice covered a portion of the earth. Geological evidence points to a brief episode of widespread glaciation that covered a part of the southern hemisphere some 200 million years before—a mere prelude to eventual cooling of the earth. But the Pleistocene brought an entire series of continental ice sheets out of what is now Canada, each followed by an interglacial retreat. For all we can guess, there may be similar invasions in the future.

After the first approach of glaciation, the Meramec was threatened three more times but was never touched by any glacier. Each attack of the massive ice sheet inched its way southward, over many centuries, to a frontier where its melting became faster than its advance. Then it pulled back for a few thousand years. Each glacier was the result of heavy snows piling up far to the north, then becoming compacted into ice. As with torrential rain that gathers into a river to cause its worst flooding far downstream, each advance was pushed along far beyond its frigid place of origin. Each glacial thrust was, in effect, a broad river of ice whose leading edge reached a warm climate and melted.

Of the four advances, the last came closest to the Meramec; it left granitic rubble just fifty miles to the north. Local drainages were no doubt affected, but not enough to destroy the hills and valley that the Meramec had already carved. Subterranean passages were well charged with icy, mud-laden water from the glacier frontier not far away; it must have been a time of many great, gushing springs. The deciduous forest and animal community of the watershed were forced to move southward, as though in an autumn migration, and to return many generations later as the ice retreated. The great mass of ice that periodically built up to the north may have had subtle influences on these movements.

Our limited perception of time tries to tell us that the earth's crust is firm and immovable, but we know that on a continental scale it is not. Broad, vulnerable plates of it bulge in places, yield in others, and sometimes even overlap. Earthquakes are typical reminders of such movements. Portions of the crust, more or less floating on a pliable core, may bulge upward as a result of some downward force upon an adjacent region. Thus it is conceivable that the last uplifting of the Meramec's foundations was influenced by the Ice Age. Repeated accumulations of glacial ice to the north must have exerted tremendous pressures that had to be compensated somewhere; that somewhere may be the present Ozark Plateau. But if this is so, it had to be an extremely slow process, as slow as the accumulation of thousands of feet of glacial ice upon the northern states and Canada. As we already know, the Meramec was not altered as by a sudden tilting but was gradually elevated until it entrenched itself within previously developed meanders.

All of this had its influence, of course, on the Meramec's plant and animal communities. At the onset of the Pleistocene epoch we would have seen a landscape eroded to gentle contours, with low hills flanking a broad valley through which channels meandered in swampy undulations. There, in the temporary lowlands, were groves of trees suited to a poorly drained environment; they were as extensive as those adapted to drier conditions in the hills. As the landscape once more became elevated and better drained, however, the ratio of forest types was changed. Lowland trees such as sycamores, willows, cottonwoods, silver maple, and swamp-loving oaks—except in the newly entrenched valley—yielded to ridge-type oaks, hickories, and the cedars that now grace the hills. While this happened quite recently in terms of geologic time, it left us with no evidence except whatever identifiable pollen grains are exhumed by paleobotanists from buried sediments of the time. The more easily recognizable portions of trees simply rotted away with time. The Meramec's Pleistocene mammals and their solid bones have left us with a considerable record of their passing, however.

Tapirs, sloths, wolves, bison, peccaries, and elephantlike beasts now extinct in the Meramec basin—along with species still existing—occasionally stumbled into swampy pits, floundered, and suffocated in the muck. Their accumulated bones have been unearthed at excavated ponds in uplands that were the lowlands of interglacial periods. Others have been found in the rubble of sinkholes. Remains of a variety of mammals have been discovered in the mud of Meramec-basin caves; there the beasts entered, probably seeking shelter from enemies or cold, and then died. Some bones have even been exposed by the shifting of gravelbars within local channels. An abundant record is available, telling us that quite a few mammal species perished forever during the Ice Age, whether due to climatic stress or other less obvious factors. Among them were the ones already mentioned, including those elephantlike beasts known specifically as the woolly mammoth and the mastodon, whose remains, wherever found, easily attract attention because they are so massive. Mammoths were adapted to cool, open terrains such as probably existed between glacial frontiers and woodlands. They wore heavy coats of coarse, ragged fur. Their teeth, each one large enough to fill a man's palm, were corrugated in cross-section like those of a horse and suggest that they grazed on a diet of low plants, such as herbs and grasses. They were probably at the southern edge of their range during glacial advances, and their record is scant in the Ozark region. Mastodons, on the other hand, must have been quite common judging from the widespread abundance of their remains. They were not as hairy as mammoths, and their teeth, while similar in size, were capped by double rows of rounded points, each larger than a single human tooth. These cusps helped them to grind such coarse material as leaf-covered twigs ripped off of trees and bushes. Obviously they were dwellers of the woodlands until they finally became extinct.

The Ice Age took a heavy toll in animal lives, as did the mysterious changes of earlier times with the destruction of abundant trilobites of the primordial sea, fern forests of the coal age, and giant reptiles of a later period. But each dramatic upheaval in the earth's ever-changing patterns of life created a wealth of new species and spared others from extinction. Experiments in nature do not necessarily replace the old, as many species survive in a continuing expansion of living diversity. The world of the Meramec tells its own story in this respect.

4   Community of the Meramec

Four times in recent geological history the Meramec was threatened by continental glaciation. Each frigid advance forced native plant and animal communities southward, as though to send them into exile, while other life forms invaded from the north to take their places. Each retreat of a glacier then allowed the natives a slow return, at least most of them. The stresses of environmental change during these cycles caused many casualties, including the extinction of huge, cumbersome mammals such as mastodons and woolly mammoths. New species of plants and animals must also have evolved, however, especially smaller forms with short generation spans to allow quicker adaptation. The Meramec's diversity of life surely benefited from these changes.

It was also enriched over the centuries by other influences, among them topography and climate. Steep hills of the present-day watershed slope off to various compass directions, depending on local drainage patterns. The sun, however, always shines from the south; its angle of repose above the horizon changes with the seasons but always from the same general direction. This results in hotter and drier conditions on south-facing slopes than on those tilting northward. Plants and animals reflect these local differences, and this too adds to the overall diversity. A scrubby oak facing the hot summer sun does not share its place with a basswood tree, which needs a shaded environment. A sun-loving lizard scurrying after insects on a southern slope is, in terms of needs, far removed from a salamander slinking in moss-bedded coolness on the opposite slope. Variety of life is also enhanced by the position of the Ozark hills in an east-west climatic transition zone. Westward is a drier climate, with diminishing woodlands merging into prairie; eastward are more humid conditions and denser forestland. The sum of these factors, in terms of the Meramec, adds up to a fascinating assortment of life.

The entire watershed of four thousand square miles, smaller than the state of Connecticut, supports well over a thousand types of flowering plants, from the tiniest duckweed to the largest sycamore tree. It provides haven for more than two hundred species of birds, in appropriate season, from wintering bald eagles to summering hummingbirds. It is permanent home to some sixty different mammals plus fifty reptiles. There is no way to count the species of insects that teem in the hills and the valley during a single growing season. Waters of the Meramec and its tributaries harbor a hundred species of fish, give birth to thirty kinds of amphibians, and provide a scavenging bed for at least forty identifiable types of lowly mussels. Among these are a certain number of rare and potentially endangered life forms. Such an accounting might be impressive to incurable listers, but it really tells nothing about the relationship among varied forms of life. It is not a who's who of the natural community; it does not explain the role, or niche, fulfilled by a single species.

Every species is but one strand in an intricately woven fabric. The entire living creation is patterned from inorganic materials of rock and soil, of air and water. It is secured at every connecting point, at every stitch, with energy captured from sunlight by chlorophyll and distributed through vegetarians, predators, parasites, and decomposers. Every transfer of energy, as when one animal eats another, is a plucking of adjoining strands. It generates the kinds of vibrations that scramble molecules of the eaten, transmitting them to other strands through additional food chains. In this sense the community is a seamless garment that clothes the entire landscape with life.

While the tug of certain strands upon each other modulates their vibrations, all of them are joined in a harmonious way. They reverberate, however gently or forcibly, through the entire Meramec basin from its aquatic depths to the hardscrabble ridges above. And they bounce back among themselves, as when an aquatic snail feeding on algae is gulped down by a

A sycamore spreads its limbs over the stream.

fish that is plucked from the shallows by a heron, whose nestful of gawky youngsters will soon be able to fly down and make their own ripples upon the water. Similar algae, snails, and fish will also yield their substance and energy to other strands of the fabric as they are eaten. Each life form may be viewed as a vibrant instrument in the symphony of the living community. The scope of relationships might be better appreciated if we consider just one of the Meramec's leading citizens—a large tree, for example—and follow its sphere of influences. We could choose from a number of species, perhaps an oak or ash or birch, but none is more characteristic of the Meramec than the sycamore.

An ancient breed, sycamores were among the first and most successful of all deciduous trees to grace America's woodlands, evolving long before the recent Ice Age. The Meramec supports only one species, *Platanus occidentalis*, the same one native to all of eastern North America. The distinctively

beautiful mottlings of its bark, except where narrowly fur-
rowed on the lower trunk, are due to the way thin sheets of it
flake off unevenly at regular intervals of time. The crown
is wide spreading and relatively sparse, as though the tree
was making sure that its colorful limbs would not be hidden
from view. Majestic, leaning sycamores commonly border the
Meramec and other Ozark streams. Seedling and sapling sycamores cannot tolerate shade, however, and often get their
start on widening gravelbars while the channel is cutting
against the opposite bank. But they shoot upward quite rap-
idly and soon overtop competing willows, birches, and silver
maples; while they cannot outgrow cottonwoods, they usually
outlast them by many years.

Sycamores are benefactors to the bankside community. In
summer, the outer edges of their leafy crowns may support
nests of orioles and tiny warblers. Their foliage is sapped by
aphids, chewed on by moth caterpillars, and at times riddled
by other insects. The attackers, in turn, are consumed in
daylight by songbirds and at night by whippoorwills and bats.
Their fallen leaves of autumn may contribute indirectly to the
valley soil or directly to enrichment of aquatic life. The small,
tufted seeds are occasionally eaten by squirrels and wintering
finches. Similar contributions are of course made by other
trees but the sycamore also helps in a special way: it grows
massive enough to be a prime denning place for wildlife.

As a long-lived tree, it sooner or later accumulates the typical scars of old age. Lower limbs become shaded out by an
ever-expanding crown; they die and break off in strong winds.
The very height of mature trees makes them into lightning
rods, vulnerable to damaging strikes. Smaller trees occasionally fall against them, creating trunk wounds. The scars multi-
ply and then are attacked by fungi and insects, particularly
wood-boring beetles. Knotholes develop in the trunks and
larger limbs; woodpeckers chisel out nesting cavities and are
followed by squirrels that expand the entrances by gnawing
around the rims with sharp incisors. The largest chiseler in
the community, the crow-sized pileated woodpecker, may

Pileated woodpecker and young.

sound out hollow, rotting places beneath the mottled bark and leave characteristic oval pits in search of beetle grubs. Better yet, a pair of these handsome, noisy birds may excavate a two-foot-deep nesting cavity and use it for successive years. Pileateds are nowhere abundant, for they defend a sizable territory and tolerate no crowding from their own kind, but their loud, metronomic *kuk-kuk-kuk-kuk* lends a marvelous year-round intonation to the Meramec's primeval symphony.

Whether patriarch sycamores are chiseled out by the uncommon pileated or—much more likely—by smaller woodpeckers, cavities invariably grow larger by decay and by the work of successive tenants. Whatever healing does occur is always on the outside, the living tissue, and never in the dead heartwood. This lends a permanence to denning places as long as the trees can survive.

One of the most appealing tenants is the wood duck, which frequently chooses a sycamore for nesting. As the birds arrive from the South in early March, already mated, their plaintive whistles tell us that they are fretting over the business of finding nesting places. Their weaving flight takes them onto high limbs where the drake, handsomest of all American ducks, awaits patiently while his hen carefully inspects every potential cavity. Good ones are hard to find. Some are too small to enter; others may already be occupied by squirrels or owls; still others must be rejected if their entrances are big enough to invite marauding raccoons. Of less importance, surprisingly, is the height of the cavity above ground and the distance of the tree from water; it may be several hundred feet from the stream bank.

A sycamore will serve the needs of the hen for about six weeks; that is how long it takes to lay a dozen or more eggs, one per day, and to incubate them. A final and most crucial day of this period occurs the morning after all the ducklings are hatched and their down is dried. It is now time for the little fellows to greet a hostile world, to leave the security of the sycamore nest. The hen positions herself on the ground below the cavity and coaxes them with soft clucking sounds. It usually takes a while for them to react, but her refusal to fly back up finally registers; they sense the risk of desertion. Excitedly they begin scrambling up the inner cavity wall, aided by sharp claws and jumping motions, competing among themselves with a sense of urgency. Each one, as it reaches the rim and faces the world, pauses only momentarily before leaping. The height does not matter; whether they must fall ten feet or fifty, they land hard, but they are saved by light weight and soft bones. When the entire brood finally assembles below, the hen begins leading them to water. Regardless of the dis-

Wood ducks on the water.

tance, the risk of predation during this journey of the ducklings is far greater than the trauma of their jump.

By the time sycamores and other trees are leafing out, in
early May, the brood of wood ducks is following their hen
through quiet pools of the stream and into sheltered back-
waters behind gravelbars. But only she is present to guard
them, for the drake never shares in family duties and has by
now taken up with other males. The hen leads her charges to

spots along the banks where they can find insects and other invertebrates. (Although they grow fast, they remain vulnerable to a variety of predators including snapping turtles, large bass, snakes, and even bullfrogs. The brood becomes smaller.) At about two weeks of age, and now moving more independently, each duckling begins nibbling on bits of algae and mealy duckweed that it strains through a serrated bill; thus the diet changes from invertebrates to mainly plant foods.

Soon the hen begins to molt in such a way that all her flight feathers become lost at one time. Until her new plumage develops, she remains flightless, but when her ducklings are ready to try their wings, she is also ready. Her mate, meanwhile, is in seclusion with other drakes and also grounded. His handsome plumage of spring is now replaced by muted shades similar to the hen's; he has lost the appeal that earned him a mate the previous winter. Only with the approach of autumn will he regain his colorful breeding plumage.

During the wood duck's nesting season, beginning with the hen's occupancy of an aging sycamore, other creatures look upon her with less compassion than we would. Raccoons are nimble tree climbers and can gain entrance to any cavity more than four inches in diameter; they can also gorge themselves on an entire clutch of eggs. The black rat snake is another climbing predator. And assuming the eggs are spared, every hatchling must make its leap of no return into a world full of hungry mouths. The Meramec's threads of dependency do not always radiate in what we might consider appealing ways.

We lament dead ducklings but feel little regret for a lizard torn apart by a hawk or for a dragonfly gulped down by a bulbous-eyed frog. Our human sensitivities reach out to the warm-blooded animal in preference to the cold-blooded, to cute frogs rather than angular insects. But a stream does not harbor such prejudices; it embraces all creatures equally. Every species along the Meramec has its peculiar niche, and there is unbiased room for any life form that can evolve a scheme for survival and the capacity to reproduce.

Consider a male smallmouth bass that lurks under the tangled, water-exposed roots of an aging sycamore leaning out over the Meramec. A tight little raft of downy wood ducks paddles close by, the mother hen leading them along the bank, where they glean insects from overhanging vegetation. Vaguely she perceives movement below the tangled roots. With a quick, gentle note of urging, she signals her brood to move on. One little fellow lags behind for a moment, one eye attracted to whirligig beetles spinning on the water. It becomes isolated. The bass darts out and upward; with one violent swallowing reflex, it has another meal.

Later, the bass scoops out a shallow depression in a bed of gravel and, by his discreet actions, attracts a female to deposit her eggs while he releases sperm with a quivering body. By this time there are certain parts of the duckling—components unidentifiable within the biochemistry of digestion—that have become part of the bass and now serve, for example, to repair a damaged portion of the tail fin that had become badly frayed in the process of its nest building. But this is not the end of the sequence; far from it. A miniscule bit of the duckling might now become part of a mussel, an aquatic, shell-producing creature with necessary ties to fish or other aquatic life.

Mussels are abundant in the Meramec basin because they depend on the same kind of ancient rock that is so important to the quality of nearly all Ozark streams. The dolomitic limestone, vulnerable as it is to leaching action and the formation of springs and caves, is a constant presence in all local channels. This causes the water to be hard, as the expression goes, meaning that it carries a high concentration of dissolved calcium carbonate, which is precisely what is needed by mussels to manufacture their shells.

The forty or so recognizable species of mussels known to the Meramec basin all function as aquatic vacuum sweepers. Each is equipped with a system of internal tubes, lined with millions of microscopic cilia, hairlike extensions of their individual cells. The cilia are in constant motion, directing suspended algae, plankton animals, and organic waste to be filtered through and into the creature's digestive system.

Mussels move along the bottom by means of a single wedge-shaped muscle, or foot, which is extended into mud or sand and then pulled back. The purchase of this appendage is rather weak, however, and its ability to pull the shelled body along cannot be hurried; it works slowly and tediously. Traveling a few feet into deeper water when drought lowers the channel or when winter ice becomes a threat can be an arduous journey for a mussel. One might wonder how the many species ever succeeded in distributing themselves all up and down the Meramec and its tributaries.

If we would try to judge the worth of mussels as living vacuum sweepers in cleaning the stream bottom of organic junk, then we would have to admit that they are extremely inefficient. They work much too slowly and their efforts are negligible, even where they congregate in large numbers. In form and function they seem to be relics from the distant geological past. They cannot see or hear as we do. Their senses are restricted mainly to feeling vibrations and tasting the water. The only visible movement they make occurs when they are disturbed in their normally half-open position; then they snap shut. Actually, however, while they are quite ancient in origin, adaptation has made them quite modern because their life cycles are inescapably tied to creatures of a more recent geological time, including the finned fish of today's Meramec.

Most mussels begin life by parasitizing a specific type of fish; they become hitchhikers. First the females release eggs into their own gills, situated along the main filtering tube. Fertilization occurs after the male ejects huge numbers of sperm cells directly into the water; sexual transfer is neither intimate nor, probably, anything more than a chance happening. Tiny larval forms no larger than pinheads are then discharged into the stream. Depending upon the particular mussel species, latching on to a host fish is a case of pure chance or of the parent helping out in some devious way. In one species, for instance, the gravid female exhibits a small flap from the rim of her shell; it resembles a tiny fish complete with beady eyes. When a potential host is attracted to this false prey, all it gets is a mouthful of larval mussels that then attach to the gills. In most cases, however, the minute offspring merely drift with the current until they contact a suitable fin, fall hopelessly to the bottom, or get eaten by hungry minnows. The few fortunate larvae, encysted parasitically for several weeks on a fish's fin—nourished, perhaps, by a bit of substance derived from a duckling—finally drop off to a sedentary life along the bed of the Meramec as filter-feeders. Their travels are over, the hosts little affected by the attachment.

We now seem to be far removed from sycamore trees and handsome wood ducks; the connections, nevertheless, potentially stretch ad infinitum. There are no loose, dangling threads in the fabric of any community—at some time or other they all touch each other in unexpected ways. So it is with life along the Meramec.

Mussels seem to give more generously to the community of life than they take from it as parasites. What little their immature forms gain from their fish hosts, nourishment and a place to live briefly, is more than amply compensated by what they yield in food to other creatures. Fish take their quota of small ones in great numbers.

The raccoon, nocturnal bandit of the stream, devotes much time to dabbling in shallow water. While its eyes and nose are ever attentive to stirrings in the night air, its nimble front paws explore beneath the surface in much the same way that a dishwasher fishes for a spoon in dingy water. Any small mussel, whether or not it clamps down on the raccoon's paw, is relished after being cracked open by a strong pair of jaws. A big specimen might be too thick shelled for breaking open and may have to be shaken from the digits, but any pain to the raccoon is surely worth the risk for a tasty meal; the same would apply to getting pinched by a large crayfish.

The muskrat is not likely to get pinched. It scoops up mussels from the bottom in a clumsier way, after the shells are closed. It presses them against its chin with forepaws, one at a

time, and swims to a favorite spot along the bank, often on a
half-submerged log, to assemble its collection. There it either
pries open the mussel shell or it severs the hinge and the two
ligaments that hold it closed; then the muskrat enjoys a feast
on the half shell. And being a creature of rigid habits, working
within a self-imposed territory, the muskrat often leaves a sizable midden of discarded shells as evidence of its work.

But what might happen to mussels that have thus been collected, shucked, and for some reason or other left uneaten?
At dusk on a summer evening, the shadow of an owl might
pass dimly over a muskrat so engrossed in shucking a large
mussel that it doesn't heed. On a second pass, moments later,
the great horned owl pounces on the rat and hauls it up to a
ridge-top oak for a feast. The mussel, already gnawed open,
begins to decompose in the warm, humid night air. Its odor
now attracts a variety of winged insects, including tiny rove
beetles, carrion beetles, and flesh flies. Some of these feed
directly on the mussel remains and others instinctively deposit eggs on it. The reward is small for such hungry, competing insects, but they never pass up a potential source of food;
no wild creatures ever do. And as they fly to and from the
abandoned midden of shells, they catch the attention of several
gray bats that fly a nocturnal beat over the Meramec. The mussel connection now passes through insects to flying mammals.

Gray bats spend all their summer nights feeding vora-
ciously on small insects they catch nimbly on the wing—beetles, flies, mosquitoes, midges, and tiny moths. By the first
light of dawn they all return to their cave, under a rocky bluff
perhaps several miles away, to a world of perpetual darkness
that often serves as their nursery.

With a homing instinct similar to that of oceanic birds that
nest upon ancestral rocks, the gray bats—thousands of them—
are beckoned each spring to the same cavern chamber. There
they hang from the ceiling so close to each other that their
bodies actually touch; they become a furry, living blanket of
togetherness. And as they fly to and from the outside world of
the Meramec, their membranous wings twisting and turning

in response to their own high frequency sounds that echo back, each individual is miraculously able to distinguish its own emissions. They are so stimulated by their own crowding, so alerted, that collisions seldom occur.

Female bats may carry their single offspring in flight, the young hanging by a nipple with the aid of tiny claws, but while out foraging, the mother bats usually leave them in the nursery. By midsummer, when all the youngsters are airborne, the nursery becomes deserted but the floor beneath is covered with an annual accumulation of fresh guano. Wherever deposited, the guano is fed upon by gatherings of tiny mites, some dropped from the fur of bats, and by cave crickets. They in turn attract their own special predators, usually small beetles. By autumn, after bats are gone and the acidity of their waste is neutralized by bacterial action, the guano becomes a garden for pallid, interwoven threads of mold. This growth brings millipedes and beetles that thrive in no other environment. Salamanders might also find their way to such biological refuse piles and explore them for edible fungus eaters.

Wherever guano is dropped by flying bats into cave pools, it is apt to become nutrient for the restricted community of an underground stream. It serves as food for such tiny creatures as aquatic sowbugs, isopods, and several species of snail. A residue may even work its way into the deeper passages of active springs. There—as in the case of huge Maramec Spring —it sustains three of the most remarkable forms of life existing anywhere within the Meramec basin: the blind crayfish, blindfish, and blind salamander, all of them nearly pure white and practically unknown to the outside world.

In one sense, however, all substance of life that enters the restricted and mysterious realm of caves must eventually return to the outside. Such is the nature of a watershed whether viewed above ground or below. Thus we are able to reconstruct the way certain forms might all connect in a web of relationships. From a hapless wood duck hatched in a giant sycamore to the belly of a bass; from a fin of that bass to mussel larvae that mature and are shucked by a muskrat eaten by an owl; from decaying mussel flesh to nocturnal insects to bats that tend their nursery deep inside a cave; from bat guano to tiny scavengers and their special predators. A small portion of the substance of these creatures may ultimately be flushed out through a spring. And if we can now stretch our imagination to visualize the original sycamore host as being rooted near that spring, getting moisture and nutrients from its endless flow, then this would complete a cycle and tie one more knot among living threads.

While this happens to be only a random sort of tying—an isolated example—it does connect life forms that tend to generate mixed reactions among human followers of the Meramec. The wood duck, for instance, is a strikingly handsome bird with universal appeal; the mussel is lowly enough to be ignored except by people who think it might harbor cheap pearls; and the bat, though truly a fascinating creature, is commonly regarded as just plain frightening. Yet each has a distinct role to play in the natural community and, therefore, a right to exist as part of the Meramec. But this description of a community neglects a major force upon the stream's survival; only by examining the impact of human encroachments on the Meramec can we fully appreciate its value.

5   The First Humans

It might be imagined that the Meramec's first people were
typical American Indians, pursuing game with bow and arrow,
possibly riding horses through Ozark woodlands or negotiating
sparkling riffles in dugout canoes. More than likely, however,
they were armed only with spears, restricted to foot travel, and
hunted the mighty mastodon. The time was roughly ten thousand years ago.

The last of four continental glaciers had already begun its
northward retreat, and the entire Ozark region was much
cooler and wetter than it is now. Even before that, many
thousands of years before, small bands of oriental hunters had
drifted eastward out of Siberia, across the Bering Strait—
which had been left dry by the impoundment of huge volumes of water in the vast ice domes of North America—and
had followed an unglaciated corridor down the continent.
These Paleo-Indians, as they are usually referred to, may
have followed the mastodons and woolly mammoths and occasionally killed the great beasts along with other Ice Age
mammals.

Nobody really knows when these people first arrived in the
Meramec basin. Archeologists who dig for clues to humanity's
prehistoric past can do no more than piece together artifacts
into a sort of incomplete jigsaw puzzle whose connecting links
will offer clues to the missing parts. A few collected items
might be dated by the carbon-14 and other sophisticated
methods, but this tells nothing about how a human culture
developed before that time. The most significant local artifact
from ten thousand years ago is the Clovis point, a large and
exquisitely crafted spear head that was first discovered among
the bones of extinct mammals in eastern New Mexico. Similar
clues to the hunting ways of Paleo-Indians have since been
discovered in Canada's Yukon Territory and at numerous sites
in the United States, including the basin of the Meramec.

The size and shape of a typical Clovis point tell something

about how it must have been used. The length averages three to four inches and the flat-side width is about an inch. It was produced from the hardest material available, which, in the Ozark region, had to be chert. It was carefully crafted by the ancient art of flint knapping, or pressure flaking, to have finely honed edges and yet be big enough for penetrating the tough, thick hide of an elephantlike beast. A Clovis point tapers slightly toward the base, has no corner notches like a typical arrowhead, and might easily be withdrawn from a deep wound to be thrust again and again. Finally, the base is distinctively fluted so that it can be tightly wedged into the notch of a bone or wooden shaft and then secured with a piece of sinew. Its cutting effectiveness has recently been proved by the simple expedient of trying it out on a zoo elephant that had just died of infirmities.

Archeologists tend to be cautious in making assumptions about their discoveries, and many would argue that finding a Clovis point at the site of old mammal bones does not offer proof of a hunting relationship. On the other hand, it might be argued that close proximity of the artifact to its assumed victim, as with any clue to a possible crime, should be judged as circumstantial evidence. And yet, after thousands of years, such natural forces as floods, earthquakes, and erosion could either bring points and bones together or else totally separate them. Expert analysis of the soil strata from which the specimens are taken can be significant. In any case, it seems that whatever is needed to prove one piece of evidence is no different from that required by any other; in this instance, the situation demands a jury of highly trained archeologists.

In 1838, a man named Albert Koch found mastodon bones and man-made tools, possibly including a Clovis point, near the Meramec's Bourbeuse tributary. But Koch was not a qualified archeologist—they were rather few in those days—and he had no witnesses to document evidence of his claim that a mastodon had indeed been killed by human effort. Thus, his discovery, while much publicized, was never given the stamp of approval by experts. The following year Koch found more bones of Ice Age mammals, but without any human artifacts, in an area close to the mouth of the Meramec, less than two miles from the Mississippi River. Other amateurs made local digs and similar discoveries during the next century. It was not until 1979, however, that a local site finally yielded real evidence of association between Paleo-Indians and mastodons. One perfect Clovis point nearly four inches long was found among some disarticulated foot bones; another, considerably smaller from having been reworked, was found touching a large bone fragment. Also discovered in proximity was a sizable number of pressure flakes, indicating that spears had been either manufactured or repaired on the spot. The hunters who left this record were probably few in number and may have been restricted in their travels by floods of ice melt in the adjacent Mississippi valley. The area has recently been preserved as a state park for potential future excavations.

Did Paleo-Indians who roamed the Ozark region so long ago dare to pursue healthy mastodons to the death or did they merely take advantage of beasts isolated from their herds by disease or else stupid enough to flounder in swampy places? The thought of humans chasing these monsters into mud holes is implied here, but could they have butchered them in such places? An even more puzzling question is whether these first Americans contributed significantly to the extinction of mastodons and other Ice Age mammals. Or is their demise to be blamed on drastic changes in the environment? The answer may be both, but in all likelihood we will never know.

To imagine how these first visitors to the Meramec actually lived, or the kind of culture they had, we can only guess on the basis of whatever artifacts they left behind. Such is always the case. Clovis points and a few associated tools have suggested that Paleo-Indians survived mostly by hunting. Anthropologists generally assume that hunting tribes must be mobile enough to follow concentrations of game, wherever that might lead them. They must be opportunists instead of advance planners, place a higher value on hunting skills than on material possessions, and share the uncertain rewards of each kill among all band members. Finally, since they need no divisions of labor other than that between the sexes—men hunt and make tools while women tend fires, process game, and care for children—they function better as small nomadic units restricted to the bonds of kinship. There has been no evidence to suggest that Paleo-Indians lived by anything but the kind of culture just described. They left no clues to permanent villages, no accumulation of treasures they might have transported about, no traditional burial ground for their dead. Those who followed them in time, probably descendants and known as the Archaic Indians, also left a scant record of their passing. These Indians differed simply in being more culturally advanced. Because the time span attributed to them is so lengthy—from roughly 8000 to 1000 B.C.—they are usually divided into four arbitrary divisions: the Dalton; Early Archaic; Middle Archaic; and Late Archaic. In general, however, the record in artifacts tells us that they improved their lot by inventing new tools, gathering wild plants, cultivating others such as squash and gourds, and becoming progressively less nomadic.

Evidence of these people has been hard to find in the silt-laden valley of the Meramec. They did, however, leave abundant records of their culture around the edge of the Ozark Plateau, where their favorite campsites were used repeatedly during thousands of years; these are indicated by vertical stratification, or levels of occupation. From all this we can guess how they might have lived where artifacts are currently scarce. The most revealing sites have been found along the Gasconade, Osage, and White river drainages of southern Missouri and at Graham Cave, some forty miles northwest of the Meramec basin. Archaic people often lived part of each year under bluff overhangs or in cave openings that faced warm southern exposures above stream valleys. They apparently did not venture deep into caves, either out of fear, a lack of skill in making durable torches, or both; signs of penetration beyond the twilight zone are uncommon.

The earliest Archaic culture is best known for a characteristic stone point named the Dalton, triangular in shape with serrated edges and corners flared out at the base. This design suggests that it was used as a spear or dart in hunting game smaller than the mastodon and that it could not easily be withdrawn from a victim for repeated thrusts. A wounded animal would have to be followed until it fell in order to retrieve such a projectile. It further hints that the huge Ice Age mammals were perhaps already scarce, lapsing into extinction, and that continued use of the larger Clovis point was no longer practical.

One early advance of the Archaic period was use of the atlatl, a bone or wooden handle used to throw medium-sized spears or darts with great force. Where or when it was invented is uncertain; the atlatl was widely used by prehistoric cultures before the advent of bows and arrows. It consisted of a handle slightly longer than the hunter's lower arm and knobbed at one end, with a deep notch either whittled or drilled into it just below the knob. The base of a spear handle was inserted into the notch and held against the tightly gripped atlatl handle by use of the index finger. With an overarm heaving motion, the hunter would release his finger at the proper instant to propel the spear forward. Extra leverage was thus provided to the thrower; with practice, his aim could become as deadly as his force.

While hunting remained important to the advancing cultures, the utilization of plant food must have increased as they became less nomadic. Late Archaic cultures depended quite a bit on growing crops, particularly squash. Artifacts discovered at their favorite campsites have often included large stones with rounded depressions, mortars, and smooth, barlike pestles. These implements were likely used for grinding acorns, hickory nuts, and other hard seeds whose shell fragments have been dug up around carbon-blackened fire pits.

Clothing of the time was patterned almost entirely from mammal hides but must have shown gradual improvements in both tanning and stitching; tiny awls, pins, and eyed needles of bone become increasingly abundant at the higher levels of archeological digs. At Graham Cave and several sites in southwest Missouri, some very careful digging has unearthed evidence of woven fabric. The coarse material, more likely for making mats or baskets than for garments, had long ago disintegrated but left clear marks of intertwined fibers impressed in fine, hard clay.

As an indication of growing attachment for certain campsites, the inhabitants increasingly used them as burial places. Quite a number of skeletons have been found at bluff sites and cave entrances; their typically flexed positions suggest that they could have been wrapped in a covering of some sort before interment in shallow pits. Although the majority of discoveries about Archaic Indians have been made outside of the Meramec basin, there is no reason to doubt that campsites from that ancient time might someday be found along the Meramec or its tributaries.

Archaic cultures yielded in time to people known as Woodland Indians, who were probably direct descendants but, again, culturally more advanced; these people left a considerable record in the hills of the upper Meramec. They were the first to hunt with bows and arrows, as indicated by points of chert that are smaller than earlier types and nearly all designed with corner notches. They began the use of pottery, along with baskets, to store fruits and other foods gathered from a variety of local plants and animals. Evidence of ceramic craftwork, some of it apparently not of their own making, indicates another important advance: trade with other cultures. The earliest Woodland people may have been quite isolated from outside influences, especially within the rugged Ozark Plateau, but their descendants made contact with more progressive outside cultures whose people yielded pottery skills in trade for valuable raw materials. These changes began to occur about the time of Christ and showed considerable acceleration after A.D. 400. One of the raw materials traded was the extremely hard chert so common in rock faces of bluffs, in talus slopes below them, and within the shifting gravelbars of the Meramec and its tributaries; it was widely sought for making projectile points and cutting tools. Another was the heavy, dark iron ore already in use for making mauls and other large tools and especially prized by early Americans of all cultures for its common residue of red ocher pigment. A third was the lead ore galena, which was sometimes used for making a black pigment. Any prehistoric society that ever developed a new line of useful products was surely not as secretive about it as we tend to be with modern inventions; the cultural advantages of bartering were then too important. If Woodland people of the Meramec were impressed with the many uses of pottery by more advanced cultures—a fact we can well assume—then it seems reasonable that the Woodlands would have finagled them into teaching the basic skills.

Archaic people of an earlier time may have prepared food by wrapping it in green leaves, or possibly in a hide bag, then placing it in a pit with preheated stones and covering with dirt until cooked. Their successors probably improved on this method by using a crude earthenware pot, inserting hot stones in direct contact with the food, then burying it for cooking. Shards of pottery attributed to the earliest Woodland people of the Meramec were very plain in design. Gradually, however, their advancing culture developed its own brand of pottery. It was made of fine clay tempered with crushed limestone, moistened and then kneaded. After the base was shaped out, coils of the clay were stacked up and then pressed into the desired shape. Styles varied from shallow bowls to deep urns with constricted necks, the latter for storing foods; decorations were minimal, usually in the form of cord lines and punctures etched below the rims before drying and baking in a bed of hot coals. Ceramic clay pipes indicated a widening use of tobacco.

Woodland people typically maintained their villages on sparsely wooded terraces well above the Meramec; hunting campsites were also established under bluff overhangs, but these tended to be in flood-prone areas and were only temporary. A number of archeological sites are known in the vicinity of Maramec Springs. Among the artifacts found there have been pottery, projectile points and pressure flakes, cutting tools, stone-ground implements, and refuse heaps of animal bones and mussel shells. By this time, the large Ice Age mammals were all extinct, and the hunted species included white-tailed deer, occasional elk and bear, raccoon, mink, opossum, woodchuck, muskrat, squirrel, and even skunk. Blackened fire pits have exhibited the dried, hard remnants of nuts and the seeds from an assortment of native berries.

Tools of the Woodland period gradually changed, but their makers did not diversify a great deal. Many of the smaller projectile points now showed notching at the corners and were likely used as arrows shot with a bow; the atlatl was no longer in use. Grooved axes of stone or iron ore were commonly used and so were flaked knives and drills of chert, but the greatest variety of tools came from bones and shells. There were hide scrapers, flaking points from antlers, pins, awls, and needles for stitching and making baskets; finally there were spoons fashioned from mussel shells. Decorative items such as beads and clay pipes also appeared among the artifacts. All of these, unearthed from sites close to the Meramec, tell us that Woodland people were not terribly far behind the historic Indians in cultural advancement.

The campsites of these people, as they gradually gave up nomadic ways, became important to them culturally as final resting places for their deceased. Corpses were typically buried in flexed positions, as with earlier cultures, but greater attention was given to the interment process, implying a growing faith in some sort of hereafter. A single large stone, or mortar, was often placed near the head and a few choice offerings (shells, small tools, and projectile points) were deposited next to the feet, knees, hips, or shoulders. Earth mounds were constructed over the important dead. Judging from the crowded position of most skeletons within burial pits, it can be guessed that the corpses and their attendant treasures may have been tightly wrapped in hide or fabric cocoons. But there is no certainty of this; in a generally humid climate, the centuries are not apt to preserve body coverings any better than the flesh encased within.

The number of Woodland Indians who occupied a village was probably no more than a few dozen at any one time; furthermore, there are indications that they might have moved hunting and gathering campsites from time to time. For example, if a particular site is known to contain a large accumulation of deer bones in its refuse heap but exhibits only fully developed antlers, it suggests an occupancy limited to late summer and autumn. There is also much uncertainty about how early people of the Meramec fared over the span of many years. Periodic changes in climate and the influence of outside cultures may have contributed to population changes.

During the late Woodland period there evolved an advanced society, the Mississippian, which inhabited the great river valley of the same name. Some of these people lived directly across from the mouth of the Meramec. They developed farming to a high degree and established sizable towns around huge and laboriously built earthen mounds, some adapted for burials and others, the largest, for temple sites. In spite of an urbanized culture they traded widely, often crossing the Mississippi in dugout canoes. Shards of their distinctively marked pottery are known from several places in the lower valley of the Meramec, especially at the sites of old salt springs and chert deposits near the modern town of Fenton. Close to Big River, at what is now Washington State Park, the Mississippians embellished a number of rock outcrops with petroglyphs that are believed to have symbolized the initiation of their youths into adulthood.

A large population of these people flourished from about A.D. 900 until 1300 and then fell into mysterious decline. By this time the Woodland people of the upper Meramec, even while isolated from Mississippian influences, had disappeared without leaving any traces. It is an odd coincidence that Pueblo cultures far to the southwest then also declined, from which one might guess that a prolonged drought in the 1300s could have been far more widespread and devastating than the evidence indicates. Some historians have even suggested that the expedition of Hernando de Soto, which brought hundreds of plundering Spaniards to the Mississippi Valley in 1541, may have been a disruption. But that incursion took place more than a century after the local population decline.

What actually destroyed prehistoric cultures of that time remains uncertain. Regardless, people did inhabit the Meramec basin in varying places and numbers for at least ten thousand years. Always adapting to local resources, they progressed from the flaking of Clovis points for killing mastodons to the crafting of pottery for cooking both plant and animal food. Each new gift of nature, each new skill was a manifestation of gods who in their eyes must have resided in the hills, in the spirit of wild creatures, in the revolving seasons that dictated their lives. For countless generations, down even to the days of historic Indians, they knew no other source. They worshipped their surroundings, and their impact upon the Meramec was negligible.

6   Pushing Back a Wilderness

The first white men ever to see the Meramec, probably from its mouth only, were Father Jacques Marquette and Louis Joliet, who explored the Mississippi River from the north in 1673. By that time the region had already been vacated by prehistoric people; it did not even support historic Indians. Later it became known that bands of aggressive, mobile Osages did occasionally visit the Meramec basin on hunting excursions but that their traditional villages were far to the west.

What brought the first white settlers to the region was mining. They arrived some forty years after René-Robert Cavalier, Sieur de La Salle, claimed the entire Mississippi Valley, which he named Louisiana, under the title of France. In 1723, from a base at Fort Chartres on the Illinois side, Philippe Renault sent teams of miners to the Meramec's eastern tributary, the Big River, to dig for what were alleged to be deposits of silver and copper. What they found instead was galena ore that reflected a silvery sheen and was actually lead. Yet this did not discourage the men. Within the frontier world of America, lead proved to be of more practical value anyway; it was needed in making ammunition. Small communities of miners and farmers thus became established close to the Big River, in what is now commonly known as the Old Lead Belt.

In 1762 all lands west of the Mississippi, including a vast wilderness we now recognize as the Ozark Plateau, were ceded from France to Spain by a secret treaty. The effects of this transfer were minimal, however; few Spaniards ever came to occupy the land, and they made no efforts to evict the French already there. The new owners did nevertheless encourage others to settle the region by offering grants of land. Surveys for these gifts were invariably staked out from selected points and projected at right angles that ignored compass directions; they were, in other words, oddly skewed. When the United States later came to own these lands—after transfer back to

47

France for two years and then final acquisition by the Louisiana Purchase of 1803—the federal government chose to honor the original Spanish grants. This is why detailed maps of eastern Missouri still show a pattern of crazy-quilt land surveys that seems to ignore all compass orientations.

Spanish grants were first offered to Americans in 1797, and among the first recipients was a Virginian, Moses Austin, who claimed a sizable tract to establish a lead mine at what was then known as Mine à Breton. The site later evolved into the town of Potosi, but Austin, its principal founder, ultimately gained more recognition as father of the founder of Texas. Stephen Austin, with paternal help, started the first American colony in that southwestern sector and became the leader in Texas's war of independence against Mexico.

Along with their oddly skewed land grants, the Spaniards left another, temporary, influence upon the Meramec basin. They enticed certain Indians to immigrate from the east, and for a special reason. Early settlers in the mining areas had occasionally been harassed by Osage hunters from the west and greatly feared their incursions and pugnacious ways. Friendlier Indians from the east were then being forced westward, so Spanish officials, shortly before 1800, began to welcome them in hope that they might fend off the undesirable Osages. The result was that for a time, until about 1818, one group of Shawnees had a village at the mouth of the Bourbeuse and another group of them, along with Delawares, established themselves along the upper Huzzah. The Osages, meanwhile, were also being forced westward; in fact, they officially gave up hunting grounds in eastern Missouri in 1808 when they signed the treaty of Fort Osage, a short distance down the Missouri River from present-day Kansas City.

By 1820 there were no Indians residing in the Meramec basin. The new people, as they were doing all over America, took over the land with an eagerness sometimes directed by a motive of greed but always with the firm belief that God considered them above all other creatures, including the natives they viewed as savages. The whites were determined to push back all wilderness and exploit whatever resources might fulfill their vision of a new civilization. Their success in the Ozarks, however, was to be neither quick, easy, nor in total accord with their goal of reshaping the land.

Even with a minimum of resistance from Indians, white settlement of the Ozark Plateau lagged behind that of surrounding regions. The isolation of rugged terrain and tortuous, barely navigable streams were major deterrents. The lower valley of the Meramec became settled after the fur-trading post of St. Louis was established in 1764; its headwaters remained unknown except to a few hunters and trappers for at least another half-century. What the frontiersmen did learn, however, was that Indians had long been attracted to the site of a great spring for its abundance of a material they treasured and also traded, a material that was usable in making heavy tools and that provided red ocher. The place was Maramec Spring and the treasure was a mixture of iron ores, mostly hematite. Word of this was somehow conveyed in the early 1820s to a wealthy ironmonger named Thomas James, who was then operating out of Chillicothe, Ohio.

One account has it that James learned of this body of ore in the remote Ozark wilderness from a band of disgruntled Indians who traveled across Ohio toward Washington, D.C., intent on complaining to the Great White Father about encroachments upon their homeland. As they trespassed upon his property, he stopped them and discovered that they carried easily recognizable samples of hematite. From his position of advantage he thus finagled a deal with them. He permitted them to camp on his land, both on their way to Washington and on their return, and he even agreed to feed them on the promise that they would then tell him the exact source of their treasure. This tale is subject to doubt, however, since the location of the huge spring and its nearby deposit of iron ore were at that time already well known; James could have gotten word of it from a business acquaintance in St. Louis.

In any case, Thomas James sent an associate, Samuel Massey, also expert in the business of metallurgy, to make the long journey from Ohio to Maramec Spring during the summer of 1825. Arriving there on horseback, Massey recognized the unique potential for both a mine and a smelter. First he noted a sizable bank of ore, a deposit of hematite that had actually developed by intrusion into a large sinkhole. There was ample hardwood timber all around for making charcoal, plus limestone for flux, both necessary in the process of smelting; there was a nearby outcrop of sandstone that could readily be cut into building blocks for a large furnace; finally, there was the magnificent flow of Maramec Spring, clearly capable of supplying all water needs and perhaps even furnishing energy. The only factor missing was a market for iron products, but the two men had already developed mining operations on the earlier frontier of Ohio; they envisioned a growing potential in the recently established state of Missouri. James was a financially solvent and daring entrepreneur; Massey was a careful organizer, a detail man—they complemented each other quite well. Upon Massey's return to Ohio, the two decided to embark on a formidable gamble, considering the surroundings of Maramec Spring: without delay they would establish a complete iron works in the Ozark wilderness.

They devoted the next winter to details of planning and preparation. By the spring of 1826 Massey had recruited the skilled artisans—none were available in Missouri—and assembled many of the basic components needed for building a smelter, a forge refinery, and establishing a livable community in the wilderness. All the gear and the adventurous workers were then transported by flatboat, down the Ohio River, up the Mississippi, part way up the Meramec, which proved too shallow, then to the site by ox teams and wagons. Arrangements had already been made by Massey, on behalf of James who remained in Ohio, to secure proper title for the necessary land. The entire advance team, some twenty men in all, arrived at Maramec Spring in September to build log houses in preparation for winter. Real work of constructing the iron works and the dwellings for arriving workers' families then proceeded during the next two years. Finally, in April 1829,

Maramec Iron Works, 1871.

the first molten iron began to pour out of the smelter located in the wilderness some eighty miles southwest of the frontier town of St. Louis.

Maramec Iron Works and its community were planned and developed with many practical, ingenious features. A low dam of earth and stone was built two hundred yards below the great spring's outlet to form a pond, called a forebay, and to divert a head of water power into any of three separate races and water wheels. These in turn activated a pair of pistonlike blowers for the smelter, large trip-hammers for the forge refinery, and grinding wheels for a community gristmill. Among the larger buildings erected were one to shelter the furnace and smelter plus two others for blower and forge components; eventually there was a carpentry shop, blacksmith shop, general store, and boardinghouse for unmarried men, in addition to numerous log dwellings for families. The project became a completely functioning company town.

Manager of the entire operation at first was Massey, the junior partner, while James remained in Ohio to oversee other interests. During the first decade, however, the two men became embroiled in a series of management problems and disputes. Trying to maintain a viable industry on the far edge of a frontier was challenging enough without the two business partners being separated by hundreds of miles. Recruitment of workers to live in a backwoods setting was always difficult, and from time to time black slaves had to be leased by the company on a short-term basis. The hauling of pig iron, castings, and other finished products to an expanding sphere of markets was a constant problem; so was the high cost of contracting for needed equipment and getting it to the site.

In 1843, a year when finances became a critical factor in the management disputes, Thomas James sent his son William from Ohio to mediate. William stayed on, and what happened after that, as might have been expected, was that the James family in 1847 forced Samuel Massey to sell out his minority interest in the company. From that time until its final closing in 1876, the Maramec Iron Works was maintained under the management and principal ownership of William James.

During its early years of operation, while constantly plagued by iron hauling problems, the company repeatedly tried using the two nearest Ozark streams. The Meramec's rather small size at the spring, its frequent gravelly riffles, its many fallen trees and snags—these proved almost too much of a challenge. A few loads of iron were hauled by wagon to a bank site halfway down to the Mississippi River, then transferred to flatboats, but even the lower reaches proved too shallow. Similar efforts were tried with slightly better success on the Gasconade to the northwest. Iron was hauled forty miles by wagon to the present-day community of Paydown, then loaded on flatboats for a journey to the Missouri River. But this route

The gristmill at Maramec Spring, c. 1910.

also had to be abandoned after several costly failures, and for the same reasons.

Until the first railroad was built southwest from St. Louis shortly before the Civil War, the primary means of distributing iron was by sturdy wagon. Each unit was pulled by a team of two to four oxen, depending on road conditions, and could haul a maximum of two tons of pig iron or finished products; if the haul was to St. Louis, the return was nearly always made with needed equipment and merchandise for the community store. Eventually, a number of roads, though hardly more than two-rut lanes, began to radiate from Maramec Spring. The two most important were the Wire Road, which followed prairie ridges between St. Louis and Springfield, and the Iron Road, which went northward to Hermann on the Missouri River; the former traced the general route of today's Interstate 44 and the latter formed part of what is now Missouri Highway 19.

The Maramec Iron Works exemplified a unique form of enterprise: industry actually preceded rather than followed the settlement of a region. Credit for this daring approach is due to the absentee founder, Thomas James of Ohio, and later to his son William. Just how much their foresight and leadership aided in opening the northern Ozarks to settlement is uncertain; the various haul roads from the Iron Works, however, were pathways to the future.

German farming communities became established along the Missouri River by 1840. Soon they spread into the northern edge of the Meramec basin, particularly along the narrow but richly fertile valley of the Bourbeuse River. The heart of the basin—the bottomlands of the Meramec proper—became settled by frontier farmers of various origins at about the same time. Here a notable connection developed with respect to the Meramec Iron Works. In 1857, William James acquired the services of a young schoolmarm from a pioneer community just west of the present town of St. Clair. While teaching she was courted by a former neighbor who had moved to California, made a fortune in gold mining, become a political leader, and then returned to visit and do business with the Iron Works. This led to their marriage; Phoebe Apperson, aged twenty-one, and George Hearst, forty-three, were wed in nearby Steelville on 15 June 1862. Phoebe later bore a son, William Randolph, who became one of America's most famous and wealthiest newspaper publishers.

Even as history graced the Iron Works in this cupid fashion, the headwaters of the Meramec, including the lovely tributaries named Huzzah and Courtois, were in process of being discovered by people already experienced in the ways of isolated backwoods and hill country living. They came mostly from Kentucky and Tennessee, some with roots going back to the Carolinas, nearly all of them Anglo-Saxon in descent. They brought with them a life of subsistence farming to the narrow valleys and loosely knit communities that soon became bonded in kinship.

Each family first constructed a log house from pole-sized

trees and then opened an acre or two of forest for cropping, the clearing hastened by simply girdling larger trees until they could later be burned. A bull-tongue plow was dragged around the standing trunks with a team of oxen, to scratch the black, loamy soil and to break stubborn roots; next came harrowing with bundles of brush; finally, the seed was planted by hand. Basic crops included corn for livestock such as hogs and cattle and a few chickens, plus wheat and a sampling of vegetables for the table. Split-rail fences, usually of the zig-zag type, were set up to exclude the animals that readily foraged on surrounding wild land. Hunting and fishing were important in the livelihood of these people, always. Their water needs were supplied from small springs or directly from tributaries of the Meramec. And while isolation from progress was an accepted way of life for the backwoods people, it also allowed them the freedom to develop their own customs and means of recreation. They were among the first true Ozarkians.

These folks who settled among rugged, wooded hills shared a special quality. Though poorly attuned to economic progress, their unique brand of American culture had to be in fair harmony with their intimate surroundings. Like coastal fishermen who love the sea even as they curse it, or western ranchers who cling to their spreads in spite of harsh landscapes and fickle climate, they grew to love and defend their hard-earned freedoms and traditions. Ozarkians became reflections of their chosen land even if they were not children of it in the same way as Indians who came before; they honestly tried to adapt their God to the demands of nature. Sometimes they overharvested the game, cut trees too close to erodable streambanks, or burned the organic underpinnings of their wooded slopes. But these insults to the land were generally small scale and seldom performed out of defiance or greed.

With a growing network of roads in the upper Meramec basin came the first villages and small industries. Gristmills to process and market the grains of local farmers were built with accompanying low dams and waterwheels on tributary

streams. Among the larger were Noser's Mill on the Bourbeuse, built in the early 1850s, followed by Dillard Mill on
the Huzzah, Westover Mill on Dry Creek, and Byrne's Mill
on the Big River.

But the basin's major industry was still mining, and it continued to expand in various ways. Following the example set
by Maramec Iron Works were other operations that used the
hematite of filled sinkholes. Among them were iron furnaces
built at Moselle and Scotia by the Meramec, both in 1849, another built at Irondale close to the Big River in 1857, and one
of the largest, Sligo, which was served by railroad and operated from the 1870s until 1922. In the meantime, as lead mining expanded within the southeast corner of the basin, another type of extraction was initiated locally just before the
Civil War. It was the open pit digging of tiff, or barite, a mineral just then coming into use in ceramics, as a filler for paints,
and as a flux in the manufacture of glass. From small workings
near the branch of the Big River known as Mineral Fork, this
kind of mining would ultimately spread like a scourge upon
the landscape, defacing it with ugly wounds.

The harvesting of timber also began to scar certain areas,
especially lands close to lead smelters and iron furnaces that
required large amounts of charcoal. But the timber loss was to
prove only temporary, a type of scarring repairable by nature
because trees would grow back. And there was to be another
saving grace. While lumber barons were eventually to cut a
wide swath of commercial boom and bust across the southern
Ozark Plateau, they would completely bypass the Meramec
basin. It did not boast the large stands of virgin pine so highly
valued for construction lumber and so vulnerable to rapid ex-
ploitation. The oak and other hardwood trees of the Meramec
hill lands were to be harvested more gradually, by small operators whose principle markets were the railroads.

Three rail lines were built into the general region from St.
Louis in the 1850s. First among them was the Pacific Railroad—later to become the Missouri Pacific—extending westward along the Missouri River and completed to Jefferson

City in 1856; next came the Iron Mountain Railroad down the eastern rim of the Meramec basin to Ironton in 1858; third was the Southwest Branch of the Pacific Railroad—later to become the Frisco—which went as far as Rolla in 1860. Each one provided not only a means for hauling wood and mining products but also an expanding use for untold numbers of crossties—three thousand per mile—to be laid down across Missouri and the Great Plains.

Great volumes of ties were hand hewn by frontier farmers who sought cash by working in the woods during winter after their crops were harvested. Their technique, whether working alone or for a small company, was to fell medium-sized trees, cut them into eight-foot logs, then square them into finished products by hewing them to proper dimensions of six by eight inches with a broadax. Their next job, of course, was getting the ties to market. Each was scored for identification and hauled by wagon to the nearest floatable stream, either the Meramec itself or one of its main tributaries. There, the ties often had to be stacked above the hazard of flash flooding until the water level was considered just right; when that time arrived, the ties were pushed in and floated downstream, either in rafts or singly if the channel was too narrow, and followed to a rail crossing or other suitable place for selling. For many years the price received for all this labor did not go above fifty cents per crosstie.

After the Civil War this seasonal occupation eventually gave rise to the cult of the Ozark tie-hacker. He was usually a lone operator whose only mechanical aids were a few hand tools hauled about in a wagon pulled by a team of mules. His work required unique skill, enduring muscle power, and a rugged individualism. Yet in spite of some claims that the best among his breed could shape out as many as fifty ties per day, he gained a reputation as a shiftless, untrustworthy character. The main reason for this was that if anyone were to question him about where he secured his trees, he was apt to answer, "On Grandma's land," an indication that he simply stole them, that he lived by an outmoded code from early settlement days: wild land was always free and open to hunting, fishing, and other subsistence pursuits.

In this attitude the tie-hacker was joined by the market hunter, a parallel type of woodsman who used his skill with gun and traps to market wildlife in local villages and, ultimately, on the streets of St. Louis. In that city, for example, deer and turkey sold for five cents a pound in 1878; passenger pigeons were fifteen cents each; squirrels, up to forty cents apiece; ducks, an average of three dollars for a brace. And while market hunting was inevitably to become a self-defeating business, the tie-hacker persisted in his trade until the day when he could haul Grandma's trees on a secondhand, delapidated truck.

Settlement of the Ozark Plateau, and of the upper Meramec basin, was sparse until after the Civil War. The population of Crawford County, as an example, averaged only five persons per square mile in 1840; not until 1880 did this density double itself to a figure of ten. Most villages in the upper basin became incorporated into towns in the decade before the Civil War, but a few not until the 1880s. By then nearly all Ozark land was under private ownership, either as homesteads or in larger holdings acquired by timber operators and real estate speculators. Meanwhile, the tie-hackers and market hunters were, for all practical purposes, doing most of their business by illegal trespass.

When the hill country was no longer true wilderness and was simply recognized as wild land, when villages grew into towns with connections into every small valley by road, then something new developed along the Meramec and its lovely tributaries. Beginning in the late 1800s, word of their recreational potential spread from the local people to the urbanites of St. Louis; it was the start of a new era.

7   The Recreation Seekers

Like other Ozark streams, the Meramec and its tributaries early began to shape leisure activities for a rural population. Consider fishing, for instance. The waters were mostly clear except in time of flood; fish life was temptingly visible, abundant, and its flesh was clean of taste. Local folks could throw out lines from the banks, from shallows next to a gravelbar, or from any boat adapted for fishing the eddies and gliding over riffles.

The ideal Ozark fishing craft came to be known as a johnboat. Its inventor, obviously a man named John, is reputed to have launched it on the White River of southwest Missouri, and from there its popularity spread like the ripples of any good idea. The prototype that guided his ingenuity was probably a simple dugout hewn from a single log. Like the ancient dugout, the johnboat is long and narrow but has the advantage of being more stable. As designed for building out of planks, it is flat bottomed, square ended, and may be up to twenty-four-feet long while only a yard wide. Three or even four fishermen can space themselves fore and aft without casting their lines across each other and, thanks to the craft's excellent stability, can work standing up. Steering is done with a paddle worked around the square stern. Johnboats were in use before the era of motors, but even today outboards are considered unnecessary for downstream float trips.

The popular canoe as copied from Indian lore was unheard of in the early days of Ozark float fishing. This was just as well; its design requirements for a contoured hull and a skin of stretched canvas made it difficult to build. Moreover, it was much less stable than a johnboat, a true fulfillment of native talent that also provided the perfect vehicle for another cultural diversion on Ozark streams: that of gigging.

Gigging for fish at night became as traditional to upper Meramec residents as the keeping of hounds for chasing game in the hills. Preferred seasons were in late autumn and early

Ozark float fishing, with guide and johnboat, 1910.

spring when the water was most likely to be crystal clear. Cresset torches, or jack lights, were fixed on the johnboat's bow, backed with reflectors to illuminate the water while shielding the eyes of the person steering. Giggers took turns at the bow, poised with a three-pronged gig as the craft was maneuvered slowly over shallow pools. Part of the fascination was trying to identify the favored fish such as redhorse and hog suckers, catfish, and bass. The real challenge, however, was being skillful enough to make a thrust at precisely the correct moment and angle to compensate for that slight deception of light known as refraction. And while gigging as a sport is still locally popular today, human pressures upon the streams have forced certain limits upon it. Now gigging is legally restricted to fall and winter, and statutes prohibit the taking of those species considered worthy of line fishing.

Any type of recreation as unique as float fishing or gigging was certain to catch the attention of outsiders. Whether this first occurred on the White River where a man named John immortalized his boat is questionable. The time is also in doubt; such discoveries are not prone to accurate documentation. The upper Meramec was probably visited by sportsmen from St. Louis before the streams of southwest Missouri were discovered by those out of Kansas City. Regardless, floating and fishing from a johnboat became a premier attraction for the elite, for those who could afford a lengthy journey by train, then by wagon, to be greeted by a hill country guide with a johnboat who would entertain his guests with tall tales and show them how to catch the wily smallmouth bass. It became a business, low key but as legendary as that of western dude ranches.

Guide service rarely included gigging trips. The leisured sportsmen were mostly summer visitors and showed little interest in getting out on frosty nights to try spearing fish. This was fine by the natives; their peculiar sport was pretty much exclusive. Gigging became an Ozark sequel to the city man's Saturday night poker club. While urban fishermen spent their winter nights shuffling cards and perhaps recounting tales of summer outings on the Meramec, their rugged counterparts were pursuing a ritual of their own under a starry sky while fending off the chill with a bit of home brew.

There were, in addition to guided float trips, other attractions for urban visitors. For years a number of farm families along the Huzzah, Courtois, and upper Meramec advertised for summer boarders in a St. Louis tabloid published by the Frisco Railroad. This was prior to widespread use of automobiles and was a means for the rurally isolated natives to supplement their modest incomes. Clients would pack their trunks and suitcases and journey by the Frisco to the town of Cuba, where they were greeted by a farmer who would haul them in a bouncing wagon to his ample farmhouse way up the valley. Here was a great vacation for enterprising urban families who could afford one, two, or even three weeks in an idyllic setting.

There the guests ate heartily of country cooking, hiked the wooded hills or rode them on horseback, shared the local

Float-fishing guide in his johnboat, 1910.

swimming hole and waded with fishing rods in pursuit of bass and sunfish. Sometimes they volunteered with farm chores; when this happened their kids teamed up with rural peers and got more work done than any of the parents ever imagined possible. The joint experiences were enlightening for both families and often served to reunite them year after year as if they were long-lost cousins. Among the summer boarders were several doctors and, in at least one case, free surgery of a less than serious nature was performed in the farm kitchen. This was, of course, long before days of easy transportation, fast living, and the threat of malpractice for medical work done outside the rigid controls of sterile hospitals.

While a few fortunate families found pleasure in boarding with farmers of the upper Meramec, St. Louisans were being introduced to its attractions on a grander scale. The beginning of this phase can be dated precisely to 1895. That spring a local entrepreneur, Marcus Bernheimer, opened a major recreation complex on 438 acres of scenic land that sloped down to the Meramec just west of suburban Kirkwood. One natural feature of the property was a sizable spring that he tapped for commercialism. Its water, though hardly blessed with any special qualities, was described as "sulfo-lithiated" and heated for health-seeking bathers; this made good advertising. The visionary Bernheimer sank a half million dollars into the project with hopes of attracting visitors from the St. Louis World's Fair, already being planned for 1904. Meramec Highlands, as the complex was named, spread around a large hotel with indoor recreation facilities. In addition, there were fifteen rental cottages, an open-air dance pavilion, tennis courts, a stable with Mexican burros and—down along the left bank—a docking facility for the resort's own rowboats and its cruising yacht.

Probably the greatest attraction of the Highlands was easy access. The Frisco Railroad traversed the property, an hour's ride from downtown St. Louis, and gladly built a passenger depot upon it. Commuters of 1895 could buy a round-trip ticket for fifty cents or a pass for one hundred rides—though good for only ninety days—for $14.75. Two years later a streetcar was completed that offered one-way passage for only a dime.

Various rates for both overnight and day users of the Highlands were kept quite reasonable and, if anything, too low for a continuing profit. After a surge of good business that peaked with the 1904 World's Fair, the resort fell into hard times. The intended clientele began to shy away as everyone from St. Louis, including teenagers, took advantage of its cheap pleasures; it was slipping into a decline typical of many recreation complexes.

Meramec Highlands folded shortly before World War I, and the only effort to revive it (with a new name, Osage Hills) fizzled when the old hotel burned in 1926. This now almost forgotten venture in mass recreation did, however, introduce many thousands of urbanites to what was then and there nearly a pristine Meramec. They would not forget, even after a world war. Railroads that already skirted both the upper and lower portions would maintain passenger service until after the Second World War; even the streetcar would offer access until 1932.

Those who worry today about a Meramec overcrowded by canoeists should have seen Lincoln beach, just five miles west of the old Highlands, in the 1920s. It was the epitome of mass river recreation, a sort of prohibition-era Coney Island for the greater St. Louis area. The beach, a sandy outwash abandoned by a local gravel operation, was on the right bank. The Frisco dropped off commuters within easy walking distance at Morchels Station. Across the Meramec just to the north were depots of the Missouri Pacific Railroad at Valley Park, Mountain Ridge, and Castlewood. Spilling over the south-facing hills and into the valley of Castlewood was a sprawling conglomeration of overnight places for summer people: Castlewood Lodge and Lincoln Hotel; semiprivate dormitories run by the Catholic Corona Club and Wagner Electric Girls' Club; and hundreds of private clubhouses, some of quality and others of claptrap construction, all perched about in ticky-tack fashion on tiny hillside plots. The beach was readily accessible from all this by a ferry that ran continuously on weekends; there was also a floating store to dispense every currently favored refreshment except the temporarily outlawed booze. And there were, for the first time, hundreds of canoes on the Meramec.

The spruce-ribbed, canvas-covered craft had earlier been viewed locally as mere novelties, but now they arrived like a huge flock of ducks out of the northeast—out of Oldtown, Maine, to be specific. This is to say that a craftsman from that fabled canoe manufacturing town arrived on the scene to produce his own brand for the Meramec. He set up his plant at nearby Valley Park, called it the Arrowhead Canoe Company, and built a thriving business that incidentally served to bring competition from other manufacturers of the increasingly popular craft.

Many St. Louisans found it advantageous to own canoes in the 1920s. They could move them twice yearly by railroad for summer storage in bankside barns and, to the despair of most train personnel, the hauling was granted as a free service to encourage weekend commuting. Operators of the storage barns also leased or rented boats of various sorts.

On any summer weekend the total number of canoeists, swimmers, and beach picnickers gravitating to Lincoln Beach was well into the thousands. Most of them were city people and totally inured to crowding; they seemed, in fact, to enjoy it. This was before the time of fast cars and good highways, public swimming pools and air conditioning. The Meramec offered easy escape from the oppressive heat and humidity of city streets, row houses, and apartments; it was cheap recreation for the masses. Those who could afford better, in the meantime, sought their pleasures farther upstream.

The Lincoln Beach era coincided with that of an expanding resort business along the upper Meramec. First was one named Bird's Nest, built shortly after World War I where the Salem, Missouri, branch of the Frisco trestled across its clear water. Next was Wildwood Resort north of Steelville; its clients were transported by bus from the main Frisco line depot at Cuba. Other lodge resorts included Idlewild, Indian Springs, and Fox Springs. All of these had several things in common: they were fairly close together, they were more or less accessible by the railroad, and they appealed especially to urbanites who could afford vacationing by the week in a catered environment. Between them and Castlewood, far downstream, most of the Meramec in the 1920s was accessible only by long hauls on roads that were either gravel or, at best, barely paved; most of it received little attention.

Despite the distance and class disparity that separated catered resorts from Lincoln Beach, the entire Meramec acquired one reputation that was hard to dispell. It was viewed as extremely dangerous by many St. Louisans. But with so many thousands of urbanites attracted to it, a high percentage unable to swim, this was inevitable. There were drownings, and they generated bad publicity. Parents taught their children a fear of it, the type comparable to loathing for such unknown entities as snakes, handed down from one generation to the next.

To encourage safety and reduce the drownings, a remarkable organization came into being in 1928. The Meramec River Patrol was an exclusive cadre of men who developed expertise in saving lives and in the instruction of water safety. Sponsors were the American Red Cross and the Missouri Athletic Club whose downtown St. Louis swimming pool served as a training base. Members were assigned to patrol various segments of the Meramec, typically by canoe, every weekend from the beginning of May to the end of September. Each man, to maintain his membership, had to log a minimum of twelve hours of volunteer duty per month. In its first year the patrol helped to save ten lives from drowning during a reported three thousand hours of duty. But in 1929, with better organization, its members could boast involvement in saving at least eighty lives. The patrol also conducted instructional services for an appreciative public until World War II nearly exhausted its ranks.

Even before the war, however, ten years of economic depression caused neglect of the Meramec's recreation potential. Lincoln Beach was abandoned and became overgrown with willows. Clubhouses on the hills about Castlewood and all along the lower valley deteriorated. Immediately after World War II came an era of unprecedented prosperity when mobility of the automobile began to lure people elsewhere —to places like Yellowstone and the Grand Canyon or to Corps of Engineers impoundments on the White and other recently dammed streams in southern Missouri. Some older people still recalled happy, crowded days at Lincoln Beach but then, in the next breath, alluded to the dangers of swimming there. The idea of dams and lakes somehow appealed to them. Younger people, those who grew accustomed to long, tiresome auto trips with their vacationing parents, were brought up, in effect, to bypass the stream so close to home. In general, the lower Meramec now was relegated to bank-side and motorboat fishing folks who simply ignored its deteriorating condition.

In the 1950s it seemed that real concern for the Meramec was limited to those habitual float fisherman and canoeists who still found their recreation on the upper portion and its tributaries. Canoes were relatively new along the headwaters but proved more maneuverable than the traditional johnboat, even if not as suitable for fishing. This influx of outsiders, however small, created problems among local farmers who felt possessive about streams either crossing or skirting their property. They often strung wire fences across such channels for convenience in pasturing their livestock. Canoeists trying to float through were apt to be chased back with a shotgun or, as an alternative, forced to pay a passage fee.

In 1954, as an effort to seek a solution to this trespass problem, two gentlemen with the names of Elder and Delcour involved themselves in a test case on the upper Meramec, near the community of Cook Station. Elder and his wife, after having launched their small craft at a legal access, floated and fished their way to a fence and began to maneuver across it. The landowner, Delcour, politely informed them that they must not trespass through his property and pointed out that it was clearly posted. The Elders proceeded anyway; Delcour filed charges as plaintiff with the Dent County Court, which then ruled against him. Delcour later took his case to a state court of appeals, which reversed the claim of trespass in his favor. The case ultimately reached the Missouri Supreme Court, whose ruling, a precedent that still holds applicable for all comparable cases regarding Missouri streams, was in favor of the floating, fishing Elders. Although the portion of the Meramec in question was certainly not big enough to be navigable in the traditional sense—that is, for commercial transport of goods and people—it had indeed been used some years before for floating railroad crossties to market. Also, as determined by the Missouri Supreme Court, it was quite navigable for floating and fishing on what had to be construed as a public resource. Since the Elders had carefully remained within the high-water banks, they were not judged as trespassers.

Some landowners still look upon the 1954 precedent as an infamous act; canoeists recognize it as the opening of a floodgate of pleasures providing they respect the banks and the privileges within which they paddle. And yet, in a sense, their right to float has also helped many upper Meramec landowners to protect their valley land from forces that would have destroyed most of the natural values they treasured.

8   How to Kill a Stream

The Meramec with its diverse plants and animals has already been depicted as a community. Its giant sycamores, appealing wood ducks, secretive gray bats, lowly mussels, and scrappy smallmouth bass represent a mere sampling of the creatures that make it a living entity. Because it is alive, however, it could also be killed. Yet one does not simply wipe out a lovely stream by erasing it from a map. Nor can its demise be compared with the smashing of vital organs or the bleeding out of a jugular vein. The process is far slower, far more insidious. People contribute to killing a stream by imposing upon it a series of degradations, each one adding to a general malaise until the stream becomes a common river with barely any life at all, a lifeless ditch.

A river—The Cuyahoga of Ohio comes to mind—can be resurrected more or less. Some years ago, as the Cuyahoga wended its way through industrial Cleveland toward Lake Erie, it caught fire from oil slicks that nobody bothered to control. Now it is cleaned up, relatively unpolluted, but will never be more than a river. So it is with the lower Meramec where commercial development dominates the floodplain. The upper portion, however, is more vulnerable simply because it has so much more life.

One way of killing a stream is to attack its foundations; the stripping of wooded hills to create hardscrabble farms is one example. Mining operations inflict a more severe injustice to the watershed by tearing up the landscape for mineral riches and then leaving it covered with mounds of sterile ore tailings. Whatever the damages, they begin as gradually proliferating cancers of blight: ugly scars upon the watershed, injections of harmful potions into vital arteries, accumulated puss from humanity's gross manipulations and fouled nests along the banks. The end is conveniently directed with a piecemeal dissection by dams. The degradation may be instigated far up in the hills, or it may reach upstream from the lower valley. The first symptoms to appear in the Meramec basin date back to an era of early mining operations. Frontier mines were typically hand worked with pick and shovel and were too small to generate extensive tailings, but they did require large amounts of wood to be converted into charcoal for smelting the ores. Timbered hills were stripped for miles around, and this triggered a quick resurgence of greenery. Mine workers who then turned out subsistence livestock to feed on a bonanza of brush were forced to control the overgrowth with annual spring fires. Most hill folks throughout the Ozarks, unlike farmers in more fertile regions, became addicted to spring burning. Each year they found peculiar satisfaction in knowing that the practice generated natural greenery for their livestock, however scraggly or low in its nutritional value. As a partial justification for this practice they often allowed that it was a tolerably good way to get rid of ticks, chiggers, and assorted varmints. What actually resulted was the unearthing of countless Ozark potatoes, better known as rocks, which then washed into the valleys and choked the streambeds with gravel. Control of ticks, chiggers, and varmints was negligible, but the idea was defended as a ritual of tradition.

While spring burning was imposed on the upper Meramec basin for about a century, its effects are now mostly gone. Years of dedicated effort by foresters dampened the woodsburning habit in most places, and nature has shown the damage to be reparable. Now the old mine ruins are surrounded with second-growth forest and the ever-present rocks tend to remain hidden under yearly deposits of erosion-controlling humus.

Greater scars have been left, however, by the larger mines of modern vintage that were excavated prior to recent laws requiring land reclamation. A striking example is what happened on the Big River, largest tributary of the Meramec. There, within a broad, U-shaped bend of the channel, St. Joe Lead Company left an extensive body of sterile ore tailings covering nearly a square mile and skirted it with a crude dike of the same erodible material. Heavy spring rains in 1977 breached the vulnerable dike, carved a gully sixty feet deep, and spilled thousands of cubic yards of lead-impregnated, toxic waste for thirty miles downstream. One might well look to damming as a possible solution to this kind of problem; it could be rationalized that all the troublesome tailings would then be disposed of at the bottom of a deep and secure lake.

Not all human demands upon a stream are harmful, of course, and floodplain farming is a prime example. Even though it requires clearing much of the valley's original forest and eliminating its most pristine qualities, cultivation does create benefits. It fulfills agricultural needs while diversifying the environment. In taking from the most fertile soil of the watershed, farming the floodplain also permits dividends of alluvium to be redeposited with every major flood; this process is particularly effective where levees are not built. It reminds us, moreover, that occasional losses in drowned crops can be repaid in due time; nature imposes her price suddenly, like a purge, and then scatters reimbursements with every passing flood. It takes a blind farmer not to realize this, or one with huge debts and no faith in nature's processes. For him to condemn the stream's occasional severity is like cursing honey bees simply because they sometimes sting. Contrary to what promoters of alleged flood-control dams have often claimed, good farmers accept the risk of crop losses if they cultivate the floodplain. They know better than to build their houses on low ground; they know that inundations are part of the price for having the most fertile land in the area.

One agricultural practice that does create scars along a stream is cultivating to the rim of a high bank, especially on an outside bend of the channel. Although farming this way allows for more rows of corn or soybeans and clears a view all the way across the floodplain, it also causes a curvature of the riverine spine. With every seasonal rise, the swifter outside arc of the channel scours the bank, eroding it, sharpening the curve and robbing land from the farmer; meanwhile, a dandy new gravelbar grows out from the opposite side. On a really restless stream, one that writhes out of its banks, old car bodies are sometimes lined up in vertical rows as a last-ditch effort to arrest the curvature.

Another rural practice that tortures a living stream is the cultivation of steep, gravelly slopes above, a common type of strangulation. It causes Ozark potatoes to fill limpid pools, encourages the scouring of mud banks, and fills the shallows with ever-widening, ever-lengthening gravelbars. This choking action may also be induced by burning the hills every spring, by subdividing them with a proliferation of gravel roads to hillside cabin lots, and by racing motorcycles and jeeps up and down slopes to create notched trails for even more vehicles. Many of these vehicles come not from upstream farms but from a commercially expanding, recreation-seeking population below, from a metropolis like St. Louis, as its people push their way out of urban crowding into the country.

Clubhouses are typically the first intrusions. The first ones are discreetly built on high ground, widely spaced, the private playgrounds of the elite. But clubhouses seem to beget other clubhouses just as the people who build them do, in geometric progressions. Certainly it is the right of every urbanite to escape the city on hot weekends when transportation is cheap and convenient, to own a tiny piece of a lovely stream. So why not either buy or lease a bankside plot when all the higher sites are taken? Why not construct an inexpensive fun house on stilts so that it will offer a clear view of the stream and be elevated above its perennial flooding?

Why not? After enough clubhouses are neatly spaced along the banks, in communal aggregations, they serve to push back the wild places and assure that cozy, familiar decor typical of all row houses. As a home away from home in the boonies, each floodplain cabin boasts its own backyard—or maybe it should be viewed as a front yard—replete with perpetual bath facilities plus the fun and frolic of unhampered boat traffic. And if by chance one's private septic tank is put out of commission by the most recent flood, it matters not; the mess

Stilt-legged clubhouses on a downstream bank.

will quickly be washed away, as will any unsightly trash that happens to find its way down over the bank.

The biggest disadvantage of stilt-legged summer places is that they are seldom built for permanency. When they fall into disrepair and become liabilities, the fun is over and it is to the financial advantage of the owners to sell them as permanent dwellings instead of tearing them down. There are always people with a jaded love of the stream, disenchanted river rats, ready to convert them into bankside slums. And by this time, other blights are also encroaching upon the neighborhood.

Gravel diggings are profitable ways to clear out bankside woods and weed patches, as well as silted fishing and swimming holes, and to eliminate abandoned clubhouses that have toppled. Both gravel and sand are needed as fillers for concrete, roadbeds, and septic tank drainage fields. Their extraction does not have to leave ugly scars in the streambed but

Sand and gravel dredging on the lower Meramec.

proves more economical when it does. Furthermore, the operator who works his draglines across the channel, and builds the necessary haul roads, is doing his part to encourage further development upon the floodplain. Sizable acreages are then more willingly sold by farmers and old clubhouse owners and thus are made more amenable to the political process of rezoning. Such places become ideal sites for warehouses and factories, especially if the proper governmental agency can be found to subsidize levee protection against flooding. What people once knew as a lovely stream has now become a channelized ditch.

But even while these changes are taking place, the ailing stream continues to serve mankind. It makes a convenient dump for trash or outlet for treated or untreated sewage from a prospering, well-fed population, and it becomes a surreptitious depository for industrial wastes. And with so many roads now interlacing the floodplain, atop the banks and over

Raw sewage pours into the lower Meramec, 1970; the hinged lid prevents
back up when the river is at flood stage.

little side channels, the area surrounding the stream offers unlimited opportunities for individuals to make moonlight trips for unloading trash. It becomes the ideal nocturnal dumping place.

These degradations are always more extensive near metropolitan areas in a stream's lower valley than they are by small towns farther upstream. They do, however, have a tendency to leapfrog. If there is need for yet another gravel digging in an area already preempted by rows of clubhouses, a more likely site is surely available somewhere up the channel. Wherever commercialism pushes back recreation, the obvious measure is to locate cabin sites up valley in more pristine settings; farmers can usually be bought out for the right price. And so it goes until complaints of riverine blight beg for new solutions, new and progressive ways of fulfilling the needs of the masses; then the dying stream is prepared for the final rites of damming.

The sequence of events leading to dams, seemingly a conspiracy of pork-barrel legislation, is always carefully orchestrated. And regardless of who really does lament the passing of a natural, living stream, everyone gets caught up in the wake.

To pinpoint the exact source of the political clout behind pork barrel would be like trying to decide which leg of a three-cornered stool is the most important. For publically financed dams, legislation must be supported by three bases: developers and their lobbyists; members of Congress; and the U.S. Army Corps of Engineers. (In the western states, the Corps may be replaced by the Bureau of Reclamation.) The three mutually balance and sustain each other in a way that would be impossible with a four-legged structure; the power and stability of a triangle is exemplified throughout.

Developers are often instigators of the sequence; among them are real estate speculators, building contractors and related labor unions, and local financial institutions. Industrialists who seek to build plants on the stream's level floodplain have a particularly big stake. The land they covet is often cheaper than higher ground simply because it is flood prone;

An abandoned automobile on the bank may help to prevent erosion, but it mars the natural beauty of the stream.

its development therefore involves a calculated risk. At this point, of course, the Corps of Engineers gets involved. By virtue of special training and devotion to progress, its experts are ready and eager to formulate plans for dams, and perhaps levees, that should guarantee protection against devastating floods. To developers, however, the goals are jobs and money.

Industrialists whom the engineers are hoping to please are encouraged by dreams of having natural floods controlled, so they plan more valley development. Original wishes thus grow into necessities. And while some people may lament the loss of a natural stream, and wish to fight what they see as a conspiracy, dam proponents always have a financial advantage and, therefore, the motivation to work harder. They learn from others who have gotten dams built in other watersheds and in other states, so that they can put forward their best strategies in seeking public support.

First, the Corps of Engineers formulates a detailed plan that shows how everyone can benefit from dams. A series of all-day hearings is then arranged in selected communities within the watershed, each properly publicized according to dictates of governmental procedure. Political leaders and the press are urged to attend. The district colonel of the Corps is

to be master of ceremonies; his military uniform and de-
meanor will likely evoke respect from those present who
serve in the armed forces. Format of the hearings is standard:
plans for the dams, and perhaps levees, are offered in broad,
sweeping terms; statistics outlining the projected financial
benefits of flood control, recreation, water supply, even wildlife values are presented by a cadre of civilian experts. After
this testimony, the meeting is open to public comment with
the promise that it will all go into congressional record.

It is past midmorning by the time the Corps has presented
all the plans. Now for the testimony. Because proponents
have done the groundwork and instigated the process, they
are heard first. Leading off is a banker who decries the unfortunate problems of the stream and its devastating floods and
then, with a positive approach, praises the Corps of Engineers for its expertise and foresight in planning viable solutions; he is then followed by a succession of local chambers
of commerce presidents who repeat the same theme in different, imaginative ways. Next, an official from a construction
union shouts into the microphone that his men have got to
have jobs. There is loud applause. A real estate agent dwells
on the recreational advantages of public lakes where thousands of people can enjoy camping, boating, water skiing,
swimming, and quality fishing. This argument brings forth a
motorboat salesman to testify that his customers are forever
wanting to know where there are public lakes for their boats;
the Corps can surely supply these needs and do a good job.
Next, waxing eloquently about his love of the outdoors and his
belief in good conservation, a man refers to the disappearance
of wildlife from the blighted stream but has to admit that people are more important than birds and animals; he argues that
we need the dam. And so it goes with supportive comments
until the lunch break.

The afternoon attendance is visibly lower. To begin, the
colonel makes a plea for everybody to keep his testimony as
brief as possible so that nobody will be deprived of the opportunity. Apologetically, he makes the point that he may need to

impose a time limit. Additional proponents of the Corps's plan still must be heard and, cumulatively, they take up another hour. More of the crowd disperses.

Finally, it is time for opposing testimony. The banker had to leave for important business and so is not present when a farmer from up the valley states that he can tolerate floods but, by damn, the government has no right to take his land away to make a lake for motorboats. There is applause, yet if it were metered it would register about half the volume of the morning's spontaneous outbursts. A canoeist complains that a worthwhile type of recreation, floating a free-flowing stream, would be eliminated by the building of dams. A rural man gripes that hunting will be ruined in the valley and that a big lake would only bring trashy people out from the city. He is booed and the colonel asks for quiet. An avowed nature enthusiast argues that birds, frogs, and other wild, native creatures have just as much right to the stream as people who come out to enjoy it; a loud voice in the back asks why doesn't he go to bed with the little critters. There is raucous laughter. The colonel warns that the next person to interrupt with such rude comments will have to be removed from the hall. More people leave the hall, some in digust.

Testimony against dams is heard from representatives of several environmental groups, another farmer, two high school students accompanied by their teacher, and a professional biologist who makes a point of explaining that he is appearing strictly on his own behalf as a private citizen. It is late afternoon and everyone is weary. A final comment is allowed; it turns out to be a timid soul who has finally mustered enough courage to stand and make a statement in opposition. The colonel concludes the hearing by thanking everyone who has contributed and by reassuring them that all commentary will go into the record.

This hearing, along with the others, makes it apparent that a majority of interests in the basin favor the Corps's comprehensive plan. Abundant, supportive testimony is now in the official record. The district congressman, while unable to attend every session, had an assistant present at all times to assess the mood. Next comes a reasonable waiting period, perhaps several months, while additional written testimony from both sides is received and duly recorded in Washington, D.C.

It is during this interim that the powerful troika is completed. The congressman in whose district a particular dam is to be located tries to be as objective as possible in assessing public reaction. However, realizing only too well that a single pork-barrel decision can either make or break his political career, he finds himself under heavy pressure. He was not long in Washington before he voted funding for similar projects in other congressional districts, each one of them conveniently hidden in a perennial, whopping-big Omnibus Rivers and Harbors Bill. After committee approval, no pork-barrel project is ever subjected to the scrutiny of isolation; all have a better chance of passage if lumped together. The system works well. Besides, for any congressman to support massive construction bonanzas in the bailiwicks of his colleagues and then to reject one in his own district might make him out to be an ass among his peers. One simply cannot be effective in Congress without yielding to the golden rule of mutual back-scratching. But even beyond this bit of political philosophy, the process exerts other pressures.

By the time House and Senate bills have been drafted to seek authorization for Corps dams, numerous members of Congress have affixed their names as cosponsors. Lobbyists have already appeared in support. Learned in the ways of our nation's capital, well supplied with expense money from back home, most of them have arrived on behalf of industrialists, building contractors, labor unions, and local financial institutions.

This is not to claim that opponents of dams are without representation. Invariably, however, they are backed by only a handful of lobbyists who work for nationwide environmental organizaions, individuals besieged by a whole gamut of threats to various ailing streams, polluted rivers, and coveted public lands. Working from Washington, they may have no firsthand knowledge of particular Corps projects and their local impacts, barely any money to allocate in fighting them, and poor connections with those citizens who are trying to mount their homefront opposition against what has become a well-greased troika of political power. Records indicate that environmental lobbyists are usually outnumbered ten to one by those who support pork-barrel projects; their greatest incentive is in knowing that they champion masses of people who, in all likelihood, are a silent majority.

When the time is ripe for authorization of a stream-killing dam to pass through appropriate congressional committees, a vanguard of lobbyists has already rehearsed. They have practiced their lines in numerous, off-the-record sessions with Corps of Engineers brass and selected members of Congress. Subcommittees from both House and Senate appropriations committees have publicized exact times and places for the staging of each show. Directors and star performers have been graciously invited to be honored at genteel receptions; they crowd the expensive hotels. Meanwhile, back in the stream basin, the opponents of damming have scraped together enough money to send their own modest delegation; whatever reception they can muster in Washington will likely convene in a second-rate hotel room and take on the appearance of a wake.

The staging of each performance—formally known as a hearing—bears striking resemblance to the format of earlier presentations given by the Corps of Engineers for the folks back home. It is standard and stereotyped. The chairman, an exalted veteran of Congress, begins by voicing his appreciation for all the interest shown in such an important undertaking and warmly thanks all the folks who traveled so far from home to express their views. A brief explanation of the proposed bill is given, ground rules for testifying are outlined, and then the proponents of the plan are given front stage. From time to time, various congressional dignitaries drop in to offer brief, supportive comments between the statements of other speakers. It is a long, tough act to follow. Everything is quite upbeat, until the crowd has visibly thinned, that is, when those still present begin to yawn with weariness, and the time has finally arrived for the opposition and its negative views. But time has begun to slip away. The chairman smilingly agrees that everyone deserves to be heard but admonishes that the hour is growing short and so please make the comments as brief as possible. At this point, for all practical purposes, the show for dams is over and has been won by the proponents.

This sequence of events has been repeated too many times, often with streams having no serious environmental degradation to justify damming as the best solution to local problems. Corps of Engineer projects are occasionally turned down by Congress; typically they are not. When they are rejected for one reason or another, it is only a matter of time before they are reintroduced with minor revisions—again and again—until finally authorized. Then the necessary funding merely calls for perennial allocations from that barrel of federal largess known as the Omnibus Rivers and Harbors Bill. Projects advance, and the usual three-cornered base maintains its power structure.

In the case of the Meramec, however, there was an inherent flaw in the evolving process. The lower Meramec, where it flanks St. Louis, was already deteriorating and its valley preempted by development when its damming first received authorization from Congress in 1938. But the Corps subsequently chose to build a series of dams on the still lovely upper portions and its tributaries; when it was almost too late, a local citizenry was aroused to fight so effectively that it finally defeated the pork barrel after forty-three years of unending controversy.

9   Designs for Dams

The first proposal for damming the Meramec was a far-fetched scheme to solve a hauling problem. In the 1830s that remarkable frontier enterprise, the Maramec Iron Works, was searching for a way to transport its iron products to market, particularly in the St. Louis area. The idea of floating the stuff down to the Mississippi River on keelboats seemed economically appealing. A series of locks and low dams was therefore proposed for the Meramec but quickly rejected as much too costly and impractical because of the shallow and unreliable nature of the channel.

The Corps of Engineers began to examine the Meramec as early as 1880, but even as late as 1930 its experts held the opinion that it needed no structural improvements. This was finally reversed after some devastating floods, not particularly on the Meramec itself, but in the valleys of the Mississippi and Ohio. The worst floods ever on these two rivers came in 1927 and 1937. In 1938 Congress authorized funding for a monumental plan to build up to 243 dams in the combined watershed of the upper Mississippi and the Ohio to alleviate floods and even out the flow of these rivers for commercial navigation purposes. Among the many separate projects were projected a dam on the Meramec upstream from the town of Pacific plus another on the Big River at the town of Cedar Hill. Encompassed in the master plan's authorization was a broad statement giving the Secretary of War and the Chief of Engineers discretionary powers to refine and modify it as deemed necessary, which amounted to a free hand for enlarging its scope.

In 1943 they chose to enlarge it. The paper Meramec dam was moved upstream to a new site above the mouth of the Bourbeuse, where land acquisition would be less costly because of greater distance from St. Louis. To compensate for its smaller upstream drainage area, a third dam was added to the planning, on the Bourbeuse near the town of Union. The paper dam on the Big was left unchanged. Since all projections were still unofficial, they did not require public involvement. Americans, moreover, were preoccupied at the time with fighting World War II and had little interest in Corps of Engineers designs. The planning process therefore continued in a low key, unhurried fashion.

The Corps finally unveiled specific information on the three dams by holding public hearings near the three sites in 1949. Two major benefits were to be derived from these projects. First and foremost was reduction of downstream flooding by the controlled release of water; second was to even out the flow on both the Mississippi and the Ohio for benefit of an expanding commercial barge industry. And even while the Corps was legally empowered—by virtue of enabling legislation passed in 1944—to include recreation as a coordinated benefit, it was ignored in the 1949 plan.

It became quite evident that if each impoundment were to serve its intended purposes, it would have to undergo drastic fluctuations in seasonal water levels. Flood control and navigation enhancement would prove effective only if the entire system of reservoirs could function as a network; in this respect, the more dams the better. Nevertheless, release of water from each one would be dictated by the series as a whole. The Meramec reservoir, for instance, was designed for a fluctuation of sixty-eight feet between its maximum flood pool and minimum conservation pool. The other two local projects were comparably designed so that all three would serve as water taps to be turned on and off as needed, either to alleviate downstream flooding or to help sustain barge traffic during low flow of the Mississippi. This plan was to prove unpopular with the public because it indicated too much water-level fluctuation and hence little appeal for recreation. Surprisingly, however, its most effective opponent proved to be a local official of the Roman Catholic Church.

Monsignour George J. Hildner was prelate at St. John's Gildehaus Parish, located near the junction of the Meramec and Bourbeuse. Through years of dedication to improving the lives of his followers—most of them farmers—he became an effective spokesman for soil conservation. He also established a close friendship with Clarence Cannon, Missouri's senior congressman who also happened to be chairman of the powerful House Committee on Appropriations. Hildner, affectionately known behind his back as Alfalfa George, had a national reputation for his dedicated sermons about land stewardship. In 1942 he was named Master Conservationist by the Missouri Conservation Commission, an honor bestowed upon only a handful of Missourians, including Marlin Perkins and Leonard Hall.

Hildner became an active voice in opposition to the 1949 Corps plan involving the Meramec basin. He argued that the proposed dams would permanently inundate much valuable farmland and would leave seasonal expanses of stinking, mosquito-infested mud flats during times of drawdown for navigational purposes. He espoused the concept, however idealistic, that floods should be stopped where they start—in eroded fields, pastures, and abused woodlands—not in the mainstreams after they have already washed away precious topsoil.

Monsignour Hildner's opposition received enthusiastic backing from the Conservation Federation of Missouri, an affiliation of sportsmen's clubs whose statewide membership was dismayed by the lack of recreation benefits planned for the reservoirs. He was also joined by Missouri Gov. Forrest Smith and, most importantly, by Congressman Cannon whose district encompassed the Bourbeuse project. So the Corps of Engineers planners, rebuffed in 1949, yet without total rejection of the potential for dams that might provide recreation water as well as other benefits, quietly retreated to the drawing boards.

Floods came and went on the Meramec, its tributaries, and on the Mississippi, as they always had. The valley of the lower Meramec skirting St. Louis continued to deteriorate with urban sprawl, including the typical spread of gravel operations, wayside dumps, and substandard clubhouse developments along the banks. Hopes for getting these problems solved with federal assistance were, of course, kept alive. Corps personnel continued planning, keeping in touch with local business leaders, but also making sure that benefits of recreation would not be overlooked in the future.

In 1958, a private, nonprofit group calling itself the Meramec Basin Corporation was organized to finance its own study of the potential for water development in the Meramec basin. The ultimate goal was to promote regional economic growth and a broadening of recreation opportunities for the public. Through the leadership of its paid executive, James F. Gamble, this group managed to raise $375,000 for what it was to call the Meramec Basin Research Project. Actual work was then coordinated out of Washington University, in St. Louis. Then in 1960, to insure its own continued involvement, the Corps of Engineers persuaded House Appropriations Chairman Cannon to have Congress finance a restudy of the Corps's defunct 1949 plan; this was to proceed concurrently with the Meramec Basin Corporation's Washington University study.

One year later, in April of 1961, to test the winds of public reaction to its revamped efforts, the Corps held a public meeting at the town of St. Clair, in the heart of the Meramec basin. It had now been twelve years since the original, ill-fated plan. Congressman Cannon, already having helped to finance the restudy, was very much interested and so was his close friend, Monsignour Hildner. The district engineer for the Corps, Colonel Alfred D'Arezzo, chaired the hearing and solicited just the kind of public input he would need to justify a revised basin plan.

"Today I want to play engineers," he said in his opening remarks. "Believe me, I sympathize with you tremendously. I don't expect you to speak in technical language, but you are the engineers today. You tell me something about damages, flood damages. I want to hear something about where you would put dams, how many dams, what kind of dams. How about levees? How about power? How about water supply, flood control, navigation, recreation? Tell me what you need in a plan of improvement. You be the engineers today. You tell me. I'm here to listen" ("Report of the Public Hearing, April 7, 1961, at St. Clair, Mo.—U.S. Army Corps of Engineers, St. Louis District").

Colonel D'Arezzo had thus mentioned the most pressing issues without asking for comments regarding possible alternatives to dam building or what might be done about a badly deteriorating environment along the lower Meramec. The hearing was orchestrated for anyone interested in speaking about dams because, at the time, dams were viewed as a sort of panacea to many riverine problems.

The Meramec Basin Corporation's study, as completed by planners at Washington University, was published in 1962. Its thrust was promotion of a new tourist industry based on lake, or flat-water, recreation. Damming of the Meramec was central to its recommendations, and although it envisioned only one reservoir to serve that need, it mapped out six alternative sites. It also proposed some smaller impoundments at unspecified sites far up on the headwater tributaries. Detailed projections of potential economic benefits were given for the basin, particularly with reference to recreation; lesser attention was given to the advantages of flood control and navigation. The study was obviously prepared with deference to criticisms heaped upon the Corps plan of 1949.

Whatever technical data the Corps contributed to this study must have related to the building of dams. The six carefully mapped alternative sites offered a catalog of possibilities without any suggestions of coordination with the larger Mississippi watershed scheme that originally would have dictated all water-level fluctuations. Early responses to the Washington University report seemed favorable enough. Corps officials were thus encouraged to perfect a plan specifically for the Meramec basin, one of sufficient scope to encompass every possible benefit worthy of consideration. This plan was made public at a second St. Clair hearing, in December of 1963.

The Meramec Basin Plan now offered by the Corps went well beyond tentative recommendations as published in the

Washington University report. It projected two impoundments on the mainstream Meramec, two on the Bourbeuse,
three on the Big, twelve small reservoirs on lesser tributaries,
plus another dozen to serve as soil-conservation catch basins
at the upper limits of headwater drainages. In all, this totaled
thirty-one dams. Numerous angler-use sites were to be developed below the major dams and, eventually, a number of
levees were to be constructed along the lower Meramec close
to its joining with the Mississippi.

The three principal benefits outlined in order of importance
were to be recreation, flood control, and fish and wildlife enhancement. Another benefit was low-flow augmentation to assure future water supplies for floodplain development along
the lower Meramec and also to dilute incoming pollutants;
the matter of navigation was barely considered. Also mentioned was a limited potential for hydroelectric power development if and when demand should ever make it economically feasible. Certainly not omitted from all this was the
prospect of an improved economy for the entire Meramec
basin.

The first St. Clair meeting sponsored by the Corps was to
test public support; the second was to confirm it. Congressman Cannon, main speaker for the day, now recognized many
benefits inherent in the Meramec Basin Plan. He was amply
reinforced by the agreeable presence of Monsignour Hildner,
who was sold on the idea of numerous soil-conservation catch
basins above the headwaters and who was now convinced that
drastic water fluctuations and stinking mud flats were eliminated from the new design concept. Congressman Cannon
spoke optimistically about the plan and concluded his remarks with a promise: "We are going to provide the money"
(*Washington Missourian*, 19 December 1963).

Messages of support were read from Missouri Sen. Stuart
Symington and from Gov. John M. Dalton. Only a few people
spoke in opposition to the Meramec Basin Plan on that day,
most notably farmers envisioning loss of their valley land to

the threat of dams. The Corps's plan was now ready for its journey to Washington, D.C., and approval by Congress.

There were potential obstacles, however. A joint report from the National Park Service and the Bureau of Outdoor Recreation suggested that reservoirs did not necessarily promise the best recreation uses for the basin. Another federal agency, the Fish and Wildlife Service, reported that construction of thirty-one impoundments would adversely affect most forms of wildlife within the project area and cause virtual destruction of 135 miles of Ozark streams that supported smallmouth bass and other game fish; it concluded that such losses could not in any way be compensated by reservoir fishing. To these charges the Corps admitted having received some suggestions that it confine its works to the lower Meramec. It also responded that any impoundments close to St. Louis would demand costly relocations of towns, railroads, highways, and other local developments; these would justifiably create too much public opposition. Yet the Corps never offered alternatives to the building of dams.

State officials did not react as negatively as the federal agencies. The Missouri Conservation Commission, legally responsible for forestry, fisheries, and wildlife, was already agonizing over success by the Corps of Engineers in getting dams built on Ozark streams. For years the Conservation Commission had been seeking a balance between the demand for flatwater recreation and the equally strong desire to protect remaining Ozark streams in their natural, free-flowing conditions. Now was the time to draw a line. It would accede to damming the Meramec, thus rendering it as a sacrifice, in order to consolidate support for the preservation of other floatfishing streams. This acceptance of the Meramec Basin Plan, though somewhat passive in its intent, would later prove to be a troublesome compromise. The governor, however, took the commission's acceptance at face value and agreed. Meanwhile, the Conservation Federation of Missouri, the coalition of sportsmen that opposed the 1949 plan, also joined the band wagon. Its affiliates felt that recreation was finally getting due consideration and so gave the new plan some influential support.

The entire package—thirty-one dams included—was recommended to Congress with supportive documentation. Total cost was estimated to be $236 million and, according to the Corps's calculations, was projected to yield a perfectly acceptable benefit to cost ratio of three to one. Anticipated benefits for recreation were to edge out those for flood control by 28 to 26 percent; fish and wildlife were accorded 18 percent; water supply 14 percent; water quality, or dilution of pollution, 12 percent. (The remaining 2 percent were alloted to a catch-all benefit referred to as area redevelopment.) Actual construction was to proceed in three phases, beginning with the five largest dams. One was to be located on the Meramec itself, near the town of Sullivan and just upstream from Meramec State Park; it would be first. Soon to follow were the two slated for the Bourbeuse and two for the Big.

In 1964, to expedite passage of the plan and subsequent funding by Congress, the nonprofit Meramec Basin Corporation was reorganized into the Meramec Basin Association and its executive director, James Gamble, now became chief lobbyist for the Meramec Basin Plan designed by Corps of Engineers. Up to that time, only one small citizens group had organized in opposition; now it fell apart, resigned to the belief that pork-barrel water projects were unbeatable in Missouri.

10   How to Stop a Dam

The comprehensive Meramec Basin Plan was authorized by Congress in 1966, and preparations for constructing a dam on the Meramec were begun immediately. A minority of opponents, not entirely willing to give up, viewed it as the domino that somehow must be held up if other basin dams were not to fall quickly in place. To most people, however, the matter was settled acceptably as soon as the Corps of Engineers began land acquisition in 1968; the project was off to a good start.

At about the same time, in 1967, a study of park potential along the lower Meramec was completed by the two counties of St. Louis and Jefferson that share the channel as a common boundary. This document proposed a federally subsidized National Recreation Area for the lower Meramec valley and generated strong reactions from a newly emerging generation of environmentalists. These young people had already discovered the pleasures of canoeing, swimming, and other activities on free-flowing Ozark streams. Now caught up in the agonizing turmoil of the Vietnam War and growing concerns for a generally deteriorating environment, they were beginning to challenge many facets of the federal bureaucracy. While seeing nothing wrong with the National Recreation Area concept, they viewed the Meramec Basin Plan as totally inconsistent with it. Even as it proposed a costly effort to rejuvenate the badly deteriorated lower Meramec valley to park status, the Corps was intent on spending huge sums of money to destroy the still lovely and natural upper portion by damming it in what seemed to be a terribly misguided trade-off.

Three years after the Corps began acquiring land to surround the impoundment, a St. Louis–based outgrowth of the new concerns known as the Coalition for the Environment began to challenge the environmental impact statement for Meramec dam as written by the Corps; the Coalition soon was joined by the new Ozark chapter of the well-known Sierra Club. The document under question had been required by the National Environmental Policy Act of 1969. In this instance it was only eight pages, triple spaced, and the Corps had made no mention of possible alternatives as stipulated by the law. On the bases of this oversight and of their militant concerns, a nucleus of Sierra Club members thus decided to challenge the Meramec project; they would try to delay the construction while seeking wider support.

Their emerging leader in this effort, Jerry Sugerman, now sought to build an alliance with silent opponents who had given up, particularly farmers within the impoundment area who were to lose their land under the Corps's power of eminent domain. By 1972, encouraged by their new friends in the Sierra Club, rural opponents formed an organization under the leadership of one of their own, Robert Thomas, calling it the Citizens Committee to Save the Meramec. The two groups then sought cooperatively to bring the dam issue into public focus.

All efforts had to be voluntary and aimed at grassroots appeal. Beginning with no prior recognition and very little money, this was the only possible course of action. Volunteers began by composing and circulating papers describing values to be lost by the dam: the free-flowing stream itself; the unique caves, springs, and floodplain wildlife; the heritage of family farms in the valley. They also sought to expose flaws in the benefits projected by the Corps: the prospect that inundation of 23,000 acres would eliminate more agricultural production than might be saved from periodic flooding below the dam; the fact that maintaining water quality by low-flow augmentation, or dilution of pollutants, was no longer acceptable under environmental law; the questionable claim that somehow wildlife habitat would be enhanced. Finally, they argued that a mainstream reservoir would eliminate any chance to rejuvenate the recreation potential of the lower Meramec. Their argument on this point was that flood protection close to St. Louis, however effective, would place that portion of the valley directly into the hands of commercial developers.

Such claims by dam opponents began to arouse the atten-

tion of people new to the issue. Newspapers large and small
began receiving opposing letters to the editors; these, of
course, triggered letters in support of the project. Political
leaders, while also getting prodded from both sides, remained
aloof in their conviction that Congress had already acted in
the public interest by approving the project. James Gamble,
spokesman for the Meramec Basin Association, now felt the
need to counter the negative arguments of Jerry Sugerman
and his cohorts.

Gamble repeatedly emphasized that the Meramec Basin
Plan resulted from a long process of careful planning that involved numerous surveys, independent studies, and the input
of diverse citizens' groups. He stated that while the dam in
question was to impound 33 miles of the Meramec, it would
also leave some 180 miles in a free-flowing condition. Its reservoir, meanwhile, would help to alleviate a serious shortage
of flat-water recreation for a regional population of more than
two million. Gamble defended the flood-control benefits that,
though underestimated by opponents, would prevent much
future damage to roads, utilities, businesses, and private
property within the lower valley. The comprehensive plan,
involving construction of five major dams, was to create jobs
and stimulate new industry, especially with regards to public
recreation. The impact of its regional scope was stressed again
and again. Gamble's arguments were based on the premise of
developing all available resources for benefit of all the people.

Even as growing publicity tended to polarize public opinion, opponents of the dam were faced with great odds; Congress was not likely to consider reversing itself on a matter so
popular as public works even though some referred to it as
pork barrel. Thus, the Sierrans looked to the federal courts.
Corps officials had been standing confidently behind their
eight-page environmental impact statement, but when the local Sierrans made a final commitment to litigate, the document
was quickly withdrawn. A $125,000 contract was awarded to
a St. Louis engineering firm for preparation of a greatly expanded statement. The land acquisition continued, neverthe-

less, much of it by condemnation; preparation work at the dam site was also begun.

September 1972 found the Ozark Chapter of the Sierra Club plus three landowners filing suit against the U.S. Army Corps of Engineers. With $3,000 in seed money from the national organization's legal defense fund, the plaintiffs began an extended legal battle that eventually was to cost $10,000. An immediate injunction was sought to stop all Corps activity on the project, but this was turned down and numerous delays occurred before a court hearing was granted. While Sierrans were ultimately to lose their case, it did serve as a powerful stimulant to all opponents.

Encouragement also grew out of a related confrontation involving one of the most scenic natural features within the Meramec basin. Onondaga Cave, often touted as Missouri's most beautiful, had been operated as a commercial attraction ever since the St. Louis World's Fair of 1904. Two of its loveliest features—a growing formation of dripstone onyx known as the Queen's Canopy and a pool gilded with rare mineral incrustations in a place aptly named the Lilypad Room—boasted no counterparts anywhere. Located within the impoundment area, this cave was owned by Lester Dill who also managed the widely advertised Meramec Caverns, some distance below the dam site.

Don Rimbach, a knowledgeable cave enthusiast and employee of Dill's, now argued against claims by the Corps that most of Onondaga Cave would not be flooded by the impoundment. Rimbach utilized subterranean mapping to show that the Queen's Canopy would be nearly covered at normal pool and that the Lilypad Room, while not inundated, would be isolated from public view by flooding of the trail system. About all that would remain above water in Onondaga's high-ceilinged central chamber, nearly as big as a football field, was a pair of domed air pockets. When Missouri Congressman James Symington was eventually persuaded to visit Onondaga, he was widely quoted as saying that such effects "would be comparable to flooding Westminster Abbey."

Queen's Canopy, Onondaga Cave.

Rimbach challenged the Corps on yet another matter. It was well known that Meramec State Park, just downstream from the dam site, was replete with caves that might have a bearing on the stability of a dam. Core drillers had already been contracted to sink numerous test holes into the rocky abutments where the dam was to be secured. Rimbach personally inspected the drill sites and asked bothersome questions. Corps geologists and engineers responded at first, then became suspicious and tight lipped. They tried to chase him off. Rimbach soon sought help from Missouri Geological Survey officials who then persuaded the Corps to allow a cooperative inspection of the dam site and test holes. By this action he was able to expose certain facts previously withheld. The left dam abutment nearly to the ridge and for a distance downstream was underlain with five known caves of varying size, some of which were possibly interconnected by small passages. Evidence also indicated a cavern buried ninety feet beneath the downstream edge of the proposed earthen dam.

Corps experts answered these challenges by simply explaining that concrete could be injected into any subterranean passages that might threaten leaks; this process was often part of dam construction to form a so-called grout curtain across the entire span. Rimbach was not satisfied. He knew from his own cave explorations and from the drilling record that certain ancient passages had long ago packed with washed-in clay. In spite of whatever grouting might be done, he argued, hydrostatic pressure from even the slightest leak in the impoundment could flush out this material and create water-filled outlets to rival the largest Ozark springs. His response to the Corps was a public claim that the Meramec dam site would eventually leak like a sieve.

Prodded by the same dedication as Jerry Sugerman and a growing cadre of followers, Don Rimbach relished every chance to speak about threats to the dam and to Onondaga Cave. Most of all, he enjoyed talking informally with groups of high school students in the hope that they might influence their parents. By keeping meticulous count over several years, he was able to boast several hundred appearances before various gatherings, all at his own expense. In the meantime, his boss, Lester Dill, helped out by having thousands of bumper stickers printed for distribution; they said, in bold letters, STOP MERAMEC DAM—A CRIME AGAINST MOTHER NATURE. Supporters of the project countered by distributing their own, which said, YES—MERAMEC DAM.

In the summer of 1974, directly above whatever caves were hidden in the left dam abutment, the Corps was building a visitors center on the ridgetop. There was a new blacktop road, a sizable parking lot, and a handsome building of native timbers to overlook the dam. This $1.4 million facility opened the next year with attractive exhibits and Corps personnel to inform the public regarding construction progress.

By that time, as the controversy gained ever-wider attention, the Sierra Club amended its still-pending lawsuit, as there emerged a new legal argument: a team of biologists had discovered that the Indiana bat, a tiny species inhabiting local caves, was apt to be threatened by the dam project. Highly social at certain seasons, these mammals depended on caverns within the impoundment zone for their winter hibernation. Because they were already considered for protected designation under the new federal Endangered Species Act of 1973, there was an urgent need to determine whether their status might bear on the dam issue. So while the Corps of Engineers hired biologists to study the bats, the plaintiffs now claimed additional legal cause for an injunction.

The Sierrans and three landowners finally got their hearing in St. Louis District Court on 19 March 1975. Presiding Judge H. Kenneth Wangelin summarily rejected the arguments presented by their attorneys. In ruling out an injunction, he expressed an opinion that was common for such cases; that is, he would not pass judgment on a project already sanctioned by Congress. He explained that it was clearly the responsibility of that body to determine if a particular Corps of Engineers project was proceeding according to its mandate. Judge Wangelin concluded by saying that he would not substitute his judgment for that of the elected representatives of the United States. Since the status of the bats was still undetermined, that issue was dismissed as not being timely. The plaintiffs had sought help from the federal court when Congress seemed unresponsive to environmental interests. Now it seemed that Judge Wangelin was passing the buck right back into the political arena which had ignored them. While the ruling was a disappointment to opponents of the dam, it bought time and gained them new friends.

The Conservation Federation of Missouri, traditional watchdog for Missouri's bipartisan Conservation Commission, had now supported the dam concept for twelve years. One of its active affiliate groups was the Meramec Basin Association whose lobbyist for the dam, James Gamble, had been serving on both boards. The Ozark Chapter of the Sierra Club, hoping to arouse a core of opposition, had by now also affiliated. In 1974, at the Federation's annual convention, a floor motion to oppose the Meramec dam had triggered some heated arguments between two factions, one led by Gamble and the other by Sugerman; the controversial motion was tabled. On 23 March 1975, however—just four days after Judge Wangelin's ruling—Federation delegates again in convention brought proxies for some twenty thousand affiliate members and, by a tense roll-call vote, narrowly passed a resolution opposing the Meramec dam. It was a serious setback for proponents and prodded the Conservation Commission to begin a reappraisal of its rather weak supportive position.

The issue was now thrust back into the political arena in a dramatic way. Three weeks after the Federation vote, a group of citizens led by Emmett Schlueter who was then president of the Citizens Committee to Save the Meramec, delivered petitions bearing the signatures of forty-five thousand opponents to the state's most influential dam supporter, Gov. Christopher Bond. This gathering, more than one thousand strong, made its show on the capitol steps in Jefferson City. While everyone waited and television cameras cranked away, speeches were made by Sugerman, Schlueter, Rimbach, and other activists. Finally, at high noon, Governor Bond appeared, wearing a T-shirt and baseball cap. Schlueter presented him with a red, white, and blue box full of petitions. The governor took them without comment and returned into the capitol.

Another three weeks found the House Appropriations Committee in Washington, D.C., in its annual meeting to hear testimony for continued funding. A few opponents of the dam had made the journey before, only to be granted time enough for a brief statement by one person. But this time Congressman James Symington arranged to allow three persons to speak against further funding for the Meramec dam: Duane Woltjen of the Sierra Club, Emmett Schlueter of the Citizens Committee, and Robert Hyder representing Onondaga Cave. There was also abundant testimony in support of continued funding, as expected, and it won that day. Nevertheless, the mere fact that opponents were personally invited to speak by a member of the House was to them considerably encouraging.

That summer, Governor Bond, following an example set earlier by Congressman Symington, accepted a Sierra Club invitation to float the Meramec by canoe and to inspect Onondaga Cave. On a somewhat rainy Saturday, the governor showed his prowess as a fisherman by catching, then discreetly releasing, four smallmouth bass. He did not, however, offer any hint of backing off from his position favoring the dam.

The next event of consequence was an official removal from the Meramec Basin Plan of the second dam to be built by the Corps, a decision that came as a surprise to many people. Biologists from the Missouri Department of Conservation had recently refined a new method for assessing wildlife habitat. After applying it to that span of the Bourbeuse scheduled for impoundment near the town of Union, the biologists concluded that the valley was uniquely productive for a diversity of wildlife. Its dispersion of small farms, woodland borders, and inherent fertility indicated that at least sixty thousand acres of lesser quality hill land would be needed to mitigate the habitat loss of seven thousand acres mapped out for the impoundment. Based on this expert assessment, the Conservation Commission published a strong statement opposing the project in October 1975. This action was cheered by a group of local landowners, the Bourbeuse River Protective Association, whose members had opposed the project from its inception. In 1976 this opposition was joined reluctantly by the district's U.S. House representative, Richard Ichord, thus killing the project.

Withdrawal of the Bourbeuse link from the chain of dams was viewed by the Meramec Basin Association as an untimely setback, and with good reason. The biologists now made it known that they had applied the same wildlife habitat assessment to the area of impoundment on the Meramec; all that was delaying a Conservation Commission response was uncertainty about the status of Indiana bats and other possibly endangered species that were still under study. With the watchdog Conservation Federation now on record as opposing a Meramec dam and the Conservation Commission seeking a biological rationale to do the same, political factions were hard pressed to remain aloof.

Indeed, the only arguments now appearing to fall in place were those in opposition to dams. On 21 February 1976, while speaking to a gathering of midwestern Sierrans, including the author, at Père Marquette Lodge, Illinois, Assistant Secretary of the Interior Nathaniel Reed described the Meramec dam as a "luxury recreation boondoggle" and an "environmental Edsel." James Gamble of the Meramec Basin Association nevertheless continued to defend it, stating publicly that despite loss of certain scenic values, the dam would fulfill needs of all the people. In June of that year, however, the tragic break of Teton Dam in Idaho gave new life to claims by Don Rimbach that the local project might not hold water. Earthen dams inspired little public confidence in 1976.

That summer found politicians jockeying into position for the national election to take place in November. The *Midwest Motorist*, magazine of the Automobile Club in Missouri, polled its membership and reported that 87 percent were opposed to the Meramec dam; within just the St. Louis area—center of the project's original support—84 percent of the respondents were opposed. A later survey conducted by Navarro Opinion Research for the *St. Louis Globe-Democrat* reported that on a statewide basis 55 percent of respondents were opposed, 26 percent undecided, and only 19 percent favored the dam.

Such polls were not persuasive enough to alter the positions of incumbents for the 1976 election. Gov. Christopher Bond, seeking a second term, continued supporting the dam and would yield no more than to suggest an advisory referendum on the issue for people of the basin, which included the St. Louis area. His political opponent, Joseph Teasdale of Kansas City, managed to abstain from any public statements on the matter. Rep. Richard Ichord and Sen. Tom Eagleton held tenaciously to their support. The only major candidate to do otherwise was John Danforth, who was seeking a newly vacated U.S. Senate position. In 1972, as state attorney general, Danforth refused to intervene on behalf of the Corps of Engineers when the Sierra Club filed its lawsuit; he then held with the plaintiffs that the Corps's environmental impact statement was not satisfactory. Now he was unequivocally opposed to the Meramec dam.

After the 1976 election of Jimmy Carter (who had campaigned against federal dam projects), after Teasdale defeated Bond for the governorship of Missouri, after Danforth was voted into the U.S. Senate—only then did political currents begin to shift on the Meramec issue. Missouri's senior senator, Tom Eagleton, a member of the Senate Appropriations Committee, now stated that he could no longer support the dam without an affirmative public referendum; in the meantime he would request a delay in additional funding. Senator Danforth, realizing that possible halting of the project would place it limbo—rather than kill it—asked opponent Jerry Sugerman to take leave from his work as a chemical technician and join his staff; there, at least for a time, he would assist in planning for an alternative. Proponents of the dam, as could be expected, were immediately and loudly critical of this assignment.

Once on the job, Sugerman became engrossed with formulating a publicly acceptable alternative to the dam. The disposition of land already acquired by the Corps was certain to be at issue, recreation planning would have to be redirected, the natural features of an undammed Meramec would demand special long-term protection. Jerry Sugerman was a meticulous planner. With help from many sectors he began assembling data on the growing popularity of stream canoeing, on other recreation values, on those natural features needing protection, and on suitable land-use options for the Corps lands. This was not to prove easy. After six weeks of employment for Senator Danforth, Sugerman returned to voluntary leadership of the dam's opponents and continued refining his alternative to the dam, a proposal he named the Meramec Heritage Riverway.

While Sugerman worked for Danforth, the dam's most influential champion in Washington, Congressman Ichord, tested his constituency's support by polling registered voters within his district by mail, enclosing a carefully worded letter. He stated his belief that the majority of basin residents still wanted the dam. He argued that impounding 33 miles of the Meramec would greatly relieve public pressures on the remaining 180 miles. He explained that Meramec Park Lake would supply 207 million gallons of water to basin counties and then referred to the expected flood-control benefits. Finally, he reminded his constituents that the project was already 22 percent completed and that to cancel it now would be a great waste. Somewhat to the surprise of many people, results of his poll supported his viewpoint so narrowly as to leave an impression that his bias had worked against him. Also clouding the issue was haggling in the Missouri legislature over several proposals for an advisory referendum on the dam; the arguing ended in a stalemate over whether a referendum should be conducted on a statewide basis or be restricted to the basin counties and the city of St. Louis. The matter was shelved for a year.

President Carter, meanwhile, was hoping to cut funding for a number of federal water projects that he believed were unnecessary pork barrel. One of these was the Meramec dam. He deleted it from his first budget, presented to Congress on 27 February 1977, along with ten other Corps of Engineers projects and eight to be built in western states by the Bureau of Reclamation. These nineteen made up what the media were soon calling the Carter Hit List. Certain congressmen were furious and later maneuvered to have the various projects reinstated—all but the Meramec dam. Opponents had gained a friend in the White House.

More than 26,000 acres of Meramec project land had already been purchased by the Corps, some by negotiation but much of it by power of eminent domain. A number of choice properties, most of them originally farms, had been traded several times and their market values escalated by land speculators. By 1977, only a few landowners were still managing to hold out. Site preparations for the dam were well underway. Anticipated cost overruns were growing, partly because of caverns discovered in the dam abutments, which would require massive injections of concrete grouting. The price tag, predicted at $38 million in 1966, had escalated to $79 million in 1972, $124 million by 1977, and would surely go higher if completed. But now all funding was cut off; delays would only accelerate the costs even more.

After President Carter temporarily stopped the project, the Corps of Engineers called one more public hearing on the Meramec issue at the Sullivan City Auditorium, less than three miles from the dam site, in March 1977. A thousand people gathered for what turned out to be a circus of cheers, boos, and a rehashing of old arguments from both sides. Local proponents cheered when a woman poked fun at biologists who defended Indiana bats by asking the question, "Aren't people more important than rats with wings?" Sugerman's appearance, even though he no longer worked for Danforth, triggered considerable booing and wisecracks about his cozying up to the senator. There were numerous exchanges between pro- and antidammers.

Several arguments were focused upon to rally support for the besieged project. One of these, earlier rejected by the Corps, was to redesign the dam for hydroelectric power generation even though reputable engineers had already stated that this was not economically feasible in the foreseeable future. The Meramec simply did not have enough flow, especially in dry summer months when electricity for air conditioning was in peak demand. A more likely claim, at least for Sullivan residents, was that the dam would solve a local water problem.

The town of Sullivan depended on deep wells for its domestic water and had just drilled a new one at considerable cost to the taxpayers. But as might happen in any rock strata honeycombed with deep, ancient cave passages, this one had apparently terminated in a mud pocket. Water was abundant but persisted in being turbid. Several persons thus argued that an impending local water shortage was correctable only by building a dam that would provide impounded water. One of these was a geologist who happened to work for Meramec Mining Company, a sizable enterprise even then having difficulty with water—it could not keep seepage out of the deeper passages of its local subterranean iron mine. He and others seemed to doubt official projections from the Missouri Geological Survey, which stated that no future shortage of underground water was anticipated for the Meramec basin. It was surely easier to envision a lake than some hidden, muddy aquifer for supplying all of Sullivan's domestic needs. The water issue, however questionable, was a good local rallying point; arguments for flood control and recreation, meanwhile, were taking a back seat. The Sullivan hearing that was intended to be a revival for dam supporters proved instead to be a raucous standoff.

For nearly a year after the Carter Hit List was made public, the dam project remained as dormant as those white-barked sycamores that each winter wait along the banks of the Meramec for spring's revival. It was in limbo. Senator Eagleton had already called for some sort of public referendum on the issue; now other elected officials joined him in making similar gestures. But who would be permitted to vote: St. Louis people, residents of the basin only, citizens of the entire state? And when? Because support for the dam had been strongest in the St. Louis area, proponents wanted a locally restricted vote; opponents wanted one to be statewide. The Missouri legislature—obviously the body to decide such a matter— had previously haggled and then shelved the whole referendum concept. Now forced to act, it authorized a nonbinding referendum limited to voters residing within twelve counties of the Meramec basin plus the city of St. Louis; it was slated for the primary election of 8 August 1978. The die was cast but not without some bitterness to excluded Missourians now caught up in the issue. Two Kansas City voters, for example, in an unsuccessful lawsuit claimed that the state disenfranchised them from their rights to vote.

No political issue had generated so much regional attention in decades; news of it spilled into neighboring states. All the arguments pro and con, old and new, were once again making headlines. Of the two major newspapers in metropolitan St. Louis, the *Globe-Democrat* had consistently supported the dam and the *Post-Dispatch* had maintained a lukewarm position for it. But on 4 June 1978, the *Post-Dispatch* changed all that in the longest editorial it had published since the attack on Pearl Harbor. In a detailed statement of two thousand words, the *Post* editorial clearly enunciated a position opposing the dam.

One month later, after years of agonizing over its passive support, the Missouri Conservation Commission also took a stand against the dam. Proponents immediately charged that this sudden shift was simply a matter of political expediency. The stated reason, however, was more substantial. A belated University of Missouri report on the status of Indiana bats, with research funded by the Corps of Engineers, had just been shown to enhance the upper Meramec wildlife habitat assessment already completed by the Commission's biologists. In line with what had also been true for the Bourbeuse, these studies now confirmed that habitat loss could not be mitigated with lesser quality hill land; in other words, the Meramec impoundment would result in a considerable loss to wildlife values.

Opposition to the dam had become widespread, but the Sierra Club and Jerry Sugerman would take no chances in losing their hard-fought gains. Members and friendly helpers—hundreds of them—volunteered through early summer in a professional-style campaign directed toward the August referendum. An office was opened, a manager hired, voters were canvassed by telephone, pamphlets and bumper stickers were distributed, and free publicity was sought through the mass media. Financial contributions were received to cover expenses, but workers offered their time gratis; among them were quite a few teachers who volunteered to spend part of their summer vacations in behalf of the Meramec. Nevertheless, the most effective aid in the entire campaign might have been a professional film narrated freely by Marlin Perkins, former director of the St. Louis Zoo and better known for his nationally televised show "Wild Kingdom." The film was shown for a month before every feature performance throughout the largest chain of commercial movie theaters within the St. Louis area.

In contrast, dam proponents were no longer organized. James Gamble had already retired from his position with the Meramec Basin Association, an organization that had fallen into disarray. What had once been a formidable power base was now weak and wobbling.

On 8 August 1978, 64 percent of the voters said no to the Meramec dam. At a televised press conference following the referendum, a jubilant Jerry Sugerman summarized the event in political terms. "This makes the first time that voters anywhere in the country have been allowed to express their opin-

ions on a Corps of Engineers project. It should give Congress
cause to wonder about alleged support for other controversial
water projects throughout the country."

Missouri's congressional delegation now had to press for
deauthorization of the project in Washington, something not
to be granted easily or even willingly. There needed to be a
means for disposing of the Corps's showplace visitors center
and the thousands of acres it had acquired. There had to be a
plan for preserving the Meramec's natural scenery. Sugerman's Meramec Heritage Riverway proposal did receive some
consideration in the deauthorization bill introduced in Congress, but much of it was also rejected. As signed into law by
President Ronald Reagan on 29 December 1981, the bill offered a set of options to Missouri, precipitating months of debate among interested citizens and their state legislators. A
compromise was finally worked out, stipulating that approx-
imately 80 percent of the Corps lands were to be sold back
into private ownership with previous title holders to receive
first options. Remaining acreages—those judged to have the
greatest intrinsic natural value—were to be retained in public
ownership by the state. Furthermore, as a means of allowing a recreation corridor for canoeists, there was to be a protective easement along both banks of the Meramec; the land
involved would remain private, but the owners would not
be permitted to subdivide for the development of bankside
clubhouses.

11 Float Fever

We have canoed the Meramec in August when heat and the drone of insects make for lazy paddling; in October when golden days are tinted with nostalgia; in March when promises stir all living things. Debating which season is best might be a losing proposition. To admit a preference for floating in any season other than the present would dull the edge of anticipation; to adhere only to the present admits to a lack of memory. Yet we can agree that May gives us a lead on summer crowding, even on a weekend, and that it offers no better time for a first overnight float of the year.

Our small party includes two couples. Preparation always takes longer for that first overnight and heightens the sense of anticipation. Old items of camping gear are pulled out of storage, carefully checked over, and maybe some new ones hurriedly bought. There is phoning back and forth between the couples and surely an evening spent together working out a schedule of timing and distance from Oz Hawksley's guidebook, *Missouri Ozark Waterways*. And reminiscing about previous trips: we savor thoughts of gravelbar feasting, swimming and sunning, observing wildlife, even perhaps a stint of early morning or evening fishing.

In our eagerness to be on the Meramec, we also vow to get a head start on the Saturday morning rush of one-day floaters. We are approaching that season when canoes ply every Ozark stream like swarms of shiny whirligig beetles under the noonday sun. An outing between weekends would have guaranteed more seclusion, but that is a privilege not many people can afford. In any case, when actually drifting with the current, separate groups of canoeists can usually space themselves as though miles apart.

We tie down our two canoes on one vehicle roof and then cram in all camping gear plus four warm bodies—more than a bit crowded, but we are saving time and extra driving, having arranged for a canoe outfitter to haul us and the gear back to our put-in site on Sunday afternoon. He is usually willing to charge the same hauling fee as if we were renting two of his much-used, battered canoes. Our own two craft, I hasten to mention, also show scars and the additional marks of our own past battle. Each is plastered with a faded bumper sticker: NO MERAMEC DAM.

A gray dawn yields to blue sky as we speed down the interstate. The scene reverts to grayness as we turn onto a gravel road that tilts steeply from a ridge down to the put-in. Early morning fog has socked in the Meramec's bluffs and wooded hills; the opposite bank is barely visible, and whatever lies downstream is now only a distant current upon the imagination. A chill dampness penetrates my T-shirt, and I feel not the slightest desire to get my feet wet launching a canoe. Too much soft living, I guess, wondering to myself if the others also sense that umbilical tug of civilized living, that early morning reluctance to any thought of baptism in a cold, fog-bound stream.

As we carry gear to the water's edge, I attune myself to the crunching sound of loose gravel under my sneakers and begin to hear familiar birds of the stream: a kingfisher rattling away through fog, a yellow warbler tweeting in the willows nearby, a phoebe hoarsely saying its name under a bluff. These sensations tell me that I'm not yet hearing impaired by strident sounds of the street and the blare of television; it is still quite early, but I'm already reawakening to the lovely, too often abused Meramec.

Everything is carefully stowed into the canoes and balanced, side to side, fore and aft. Although my wife, Charlene, and I debated over which items we might leave at home to lighten the load, both of us later admitted that devotees of the Outward Bound ideal would surely have pared it down by half. State law requires every person afloat to have some sort of life preserver. Charlene wears hers dutifully, at least to start off, but I sit on mine, thinking that when the sun finally cuts the fog I might fall out of the canoe on purpose.

With unavoidable baptism of the feet, some pushing and

minor scraping of aluminum on gravel, we shove off. Just then, an outfitter comes rumbling down in his pickup, pulling a trailer of canoes and followed by several carloads of eager customers. Though we are obviously ahead of the crowd, we assuage our smugness by exchanging wisecracks about who in our group will capsize, who will get bitten by a snake, who will wash away if we get a flood of rain in the night, and who forgot to bring the steaks, beer, or other necessities of pleasure.

It always seems helpful if the put-in happens to be near the head of a long, placid pool, allowing for minor adjustments in balancing loads and in loosening unpracticed paddling muscles before reaching the first riffle. Such is the case today as we put gentle fog between us and other canoeists. Charlene paddles steadily on her left while I try to deceive her by dragging paddle on the right, steering just enough to compensate for her pulling. Any paddler can be lazy on placid water, and she knows this well, my little game not fooling her for a moment. To keep me busy she frequently switches sides; then she simply quits paddling, and we drift downstream quite aimlessly, as if in a reverie.

Finally we approach the first riffle and both resume paddling to move faster than the current; the speed assures maneuverability around gravel shoals and unexpected snags. She pulls straight back with every stroke and is ready to jam the paddle in to either side if necessary to avoid an obstruction. I use the J-stroke, rotating the blade outward at the end of each pull, just enough to maintain course. Now I spot the riffle's diagnostic V that points the way, slip quickly through it, then veer forcefully away from a sharp bend and jumble of sunken logs. This takes us past a high, rocky bluff just as sunlight begins to dissipate the fog. We both relax and I revert to lazily dragging paddle.

I steer gently along a mud bank across from the bluff to get a full view of its rugged face, to study its waterworn streaks, its cornices, and the gnarled cedars that cling so precariously to its high ledges. It is truly a rock of ages, a mirror of the

Canoe rental on Ozark streams is a thriving business.

Meramec's ancient geology. We are startled by a great blue
heron lifting from a snag over the mud bank and voiding itself
in typical response to the intrusion of its privacy. A couple of
turtles slide into the channel from a protruding log. High
overhead whistles a wood duck heading back upstream. A moment later the bluff echoes with metronomic calls of a pileated woodpecker. Our observations, while typical of any
float trip on any Ozark stream, are happy revelations. They
tell us that in spite of heavy canoe traffic and localized abuses,
the Meramec still maintains an almost primeval diversity
of wildlife. There is, however, always one question in our
minds. How long can it be kept that way?

A short distance farther we are confronted by a motorboat
slowly growling its way upstream; adding to the noise but
much less tolerable are the barks of handguns as its occupants, two teen-aged boys, illegally plink at sunning turtles.
They stop when they see us and immediately switch to toying

Canoeists enjoying the still-lovely upper reaches of the Meramec.

with some fishing tackle. As we pass they grin sheepishly and wave in a friendly manner; we find it difficult to restrain ourselves from making nasty remarks.

Below the next riffle we beach our canoes on a wide, clean gravelbar. It has been two hours since breakfast and we need to scatter. I duck into a grove of small willows and cottonwoods where I take note of assorted litter, wads of toilet paper, and worse. I refuse adding insult to previous injury. Working my way into dense brush, I maneuver all the way to a high-water bank to do what I must, but only after scraping out a pit of loose soil with my sneakers; then I cover the traces with soil, dead leaves, and finally a chunk of rotting wood. Such a ritual may seem overly fastidious, but it is basic to good outdoors manners.

By now I become curious as to what lies beyond the wooded bank and do a bit of harmless trespassing. The owner of this land, whoever he is, maintains a buffer of trees to protect the high-water bank from eroding and uses most of the floodplain for pasture instead of risking it to row crops. He also has the place posted with signs for people like me: TRESPASSERS KEEP OUT. In backing off I become aware that here is a farmer who probably has more problems with the canoeing public than with nature's floods—unfortunate but typical. His house is visible across the pasture, nestled among assorted outbuildings; it is a quaint, modest spread, in harmony with the natural landscape. To most floaters it is invisible.

When I rejoin my group, all three are sitting at the water's edge, watching the arrival of an aquatic circus. Here come a dozen canoes, all drifting happily downstream and gyrating like so many giant whirligig beetles. Occupants are laughing and screaming. Paddles are flashing in the sunlight as their handlers constantly switch from one side to the other. And now, as they begin to crowd the riffle, they all try to sort themselves and get spaced out. Too late: the current has already caught them. We hear friendly arguments among novice paddlers, jibes about just who is supposed to steer, someone asking how to take a riffle backwards. Paddles clank on aluminum; gravel crunches against aluminum; hulls of aluminum collide. The manufacturers of Grumman and other aluminum canoes remain ever thankful that there are so many outfitters renting out their products. Just across from us, one of the canoes drifts lengthwise against a log, and its occupants lean away from the impact, thus capsizing immediately. Recalling how I did that once, and how dangerous it can be, I shout an offer of help, but it goes unheard. Two heads bob their way safely downstream along with ice bucket, paddles, cushions, and lesser floatable items. Other canoes manage to get by, some nearly capsizing. Quite a show. The entire party begins reassembling ashore below us while several of the men go back to pry loose a slightly warped canoe from the offending log. Nobody is hurt, except possibly in pride, and everyone seems to relish the excitement. As a traveling act, however, it is one we care not to join, so we quietly shove off to get ahead.

Several gravelbars downstream, as we lunch on a sand bank, a different flotilla catches up. Hastily they beach their rented, numbered canoes nearby and one fellow toting a beer can walks over to talk. He informs us, among other things, that he has floated the Meramec many times and knows this stretch "real good"; he then tells about killing a deadly cottonmouth snake just off this very gravelbar. I respond that it was likely a common, nonpoisonous water snake, trying to explain that cottonmouths are more southerly in range. He tells me flatly that I don't know what I'm talking about. Just then his friends yell over that they're shoving off. As he walks away, he brashly tosses his empty into some weeds. Unable to restrain myself but trying to be diplomatic, I remark simply: "You dropped your can."

"So what," he smirks, his back already turned. "It's not your damn river." I say no more, deciding that for him the hot sun and beer apparently don't mix well.

A girl friend tells him to be a sport and pick up the can. He gets mad and yells at her to get in the goddamn canoe. I look the other way, toward Charlene, and she tells me that the girl has picked up the can. Just as I look again, he tries to wrest the can from her, but she manages to drop it into the canoe. Now the entire gang joins in to add theirs to his unwanted collection; they laugh and he sullenly pushes off. About this time I wonder if all their litter will be dumped out around the next bend.

Farther on down we pass a gravelbar strewn with several piles of trash, all quite visible as though deposited with contempt. The group that performed beer-can theatrics is now somewhere behind us; none of it could be theirs. When we come to a bridge just beyond, telling us of Meramec accessibility by road, we quickly guess the source of this accumulated slobbery. The trash, mostly cans, must have been left by Saturday-night riverine cowboys. Our on-the-spot indictment now generates a sort of drifting, floating discussion among the four of us. We debate what segments of the population are mostly to blame for trashing lovely streams. Local parties of teenagers? Urban canoeists? Nocturnal trash dumpers from nearby towns? Realizing the huge amounts and varieties of trash involved—from beer cans to mattresses and old refrigerators—we finally admit that the guilt has to be shared by many people; therefore it serves no good to stereotype the culprits. We sadly agree that such slobbery is symptomatic of a contagious malaise in our throw-away society and that we are limited in ways of controlling it. Catching the culprits, while certainly justified, is practically impossible. Occasional witnesses to such a minor crime are rarely willing to testify in court; indifference and the fact of one's own guilt are no inducements. Two options remain: one is simply to set a good example; the other is to embarrass, gently, guilty individuals and hope they are sober when we do so. It is hardly worth the effort to get punched by intimidating a mean drunk.

Our floating discussion, heating with the afternoon, finally ends with everyone taking a dip in cool, clear water. We continue to drift and swim downstream, each of us making a rather feeble effort not to turn the color of boiled lobsters. But after two lazy, blissful hours, we are overtaken by mountainous thunderheads. Rumblings approach from somewhere upstream, and we seek whatever shelter we can along a mud bank. Sycamores and silver maples sway threateningly overhead. We hurriedly put on rain gear and try to calculate the odds of a lightning strike or falling tree doing us in. Should we paddle out into the open channel? Lightning strikes nearby, and we all agree it is safer on the bank. The storm is part of submitting to the stream on its own terms; we accept this. We pull the canoes up on slippery mud and scramble to shelter at the top of the bank. By then it is raining hard.

It pours for what seems an eternity, and while we watch tiny rivulets of brown swirling below the bank, memories of past floods begin to inundate my consciousness. There was one lovely June day on the Buffalo of Arkansas when Charlene, our two boys, and I launched a three-day float. That night the rains came and proved the wisdom of our having set up camp on the crest of a high, clean gravelbar. The water rose three feet. By the next afternoon, after an almost continuous rain that added five feet more to the rise, we pulled out near a farmhouse and called the canoe outfitter to haul us out of the valley. "Sorry," his wife answered, "He's out a-rescuin' Girl Scouts from the flood and he'll pick ya up tomorrow where he told ya." That night we trespassed and camped on a rolling cow pasture, surrounded by soggy pies. Then there was my very first overnight on the Meramec, back when I was a boy at summer camp. Recurring downpours should have warned our greenhorn counselor to get us up on high ground. Instead, he directed us to sleep under our overturned canoes on a low gravelbar, next to the channel, just in case we'd have to move out. We did, in total darkness, and that was one risky trip two miles downstream and back to camp. It was years before I was old enough to realize what a foolish thing he had us do.

The afternoon storm passes, leaving an aura of calm, steamy coolness. The Meramec remains unmuddied and appealing. We slide down the mud bank like a bunch of happy otters and proceed to look for a high gravelbar campsite. The first likely one is posted with no trespassing signs; not wishing to put the case of *Elder* v. *Delcour* to another court test at our expense, we stop at the next good site. After exploring our night's sanctuary, we gather a pile of campfire driftwood on a patch of sandy alluvium. Next we haul up all the gear, including the canoes.

Some campers burden their canoes with screened cooking shelter and poles, folding cots, folding table and chairs, radio, and even perhaps a battery-operated television—all this along with necessities. Either out of slavishness or disdain for wild places, some try to bring the city out to the gravelbar, and they get about as close to nature as though in a stilt-legged clubhouse down by St. Louis. They work hard in loading and unloading their gear, dragging their much overburdened canoes through riffles, setting up and taking down, but I guess that after all such exertion, they surely need the folding furniture to support their aching bodies. Our own particular addiction is in making do with nothing more elaborate than backpack tents, foam pads for our sleeping bags, a camp stove, cooler, and nest of cheap aluminum pots. We have gotten to know the Meramec quite intimately, even its mosquitoes and other nuisance critters. If we are purists, then it is in the tradition of Thoreau—that is, by making an effort to simplify our lives for a brief change of pace. That, in essence, is what overnight floating is all about.

We have enjoyed some fairly comfortable overnights even in winter, when warmly equipped, but then the nights always seem intolerably long. A real joy of summer outings is the long, lingering daylight that extends way beyond supper. To try some fishing as the wind dies down, to take a twilight dip, to explore the evening woods, or simply to skip rocks—there are no substitutes for simple pleasures. And there is the music.

About the time that whippoorwills lash out their cadence, they are joined by cricket frogs clinking pebbles, a green frog now and then plucking his banjo string, and bullfrogs resounding with a chorus of jug-o-rum. At other times or in other seasons, entertainers might include soothing crickets,

strident katydids, barred owls, even the rare scream of a bob-
cat. No bad news on television, no situation comedies with
canned laughter, no sad country western music on the radio.
The kind of natural music provided along the Meramec is not
gimmicky or dated; it transcends the lives of all its hearers.
The campfire driftwood serves as a catalyst for us to join in. Its
cheerful fire helps to generate a chorus of our own as we warm
up to some old favorites. Our singing lends a counterpoint to
wild night sounds that envelop the gravelbar, evoking fond
memories of other floats, other nights along the stream. But
sooner or later comes the inevitable ho-hum time. Once I was
told by a first-time camper that he couldn't stand those damn
whippoorwills that kept him awake all night. My reply was
that once I had a nearly sleepless night listening to street
sounds filtering into a New York hotel room.

Float camping is not typically conducive to early rising. A
closeness of steep hills and tall trees keeps most gravelbars in
deep shade for two or more hours after sunrise, and the entire
dawning is apt to be shrouded in fog. But my own penchant
for getting up early is not easily denied. A chill similar to that
which penetrated me on the previous morning is now invig-
orating. I set out exploring and observing wildlife that the
others will miss as they sleep. A doe crosses the far end of our
gravelbar, and I wonder if she is nursing a fawn hidden somewhere in the woods. I recognize a beaver's wake as he sub-
marines back to his mounded lodge of sticks and cornstalks
against a mud bank. A kingfisher makes like an early morning
alarm clock. Invisible on some towering limb, a sycamore
warbler trails off its plaintive song. The rim of a backwater
pool exhibits tracks of a raccoon; I agitate the clear water with
a stick and arouse a backpeddling crayfish that escaped the
nocturnal hunter. I wonder how many jolly one-day floaters
take notice of small doings among the wild creatures. I hope
they do.

The others get up to rediscover how appetites are always
better and breakfast tastier on a gravelbar. No half grapefruit,
cup of coffee, and run ritual here. We have bacon and eggs

and take our time, about as long as it takes for sunlight to burn away the mist. Then while sipping the dregs of our camp stove coffee, we watch the descent of shadows from bluff and bankside trees until we are totally bathed in sunlight.

Breaking camp is an unhurried routine, or should be. We dally with picture taking, bird watching, and perhaps a little fishing. In reloading the canoes, we pack out our litter and whatever the careless might have left about—if the stuff is not too big.

In midmorning, as we drift down a placid pool, we are met by two men fishing their way upstream in a johnboat equipped with a small trolling motor. They are dressed in the local attire of bib overalls, and we ask if they're having any luck.

"Just tolerable," answers one.

"Will you show us what you have?"

"You sound like the game warden," smiles the other as he hoists a stringer with four respectable bass. They are true Ozarkians; among friends they would brag quite freely about their catches, but toward strangers they tend to be reticent. It surprises us to see these men out fishing on a canoeists' week-end, but these days they can no longer live entirely off the land; they too have jobs on weekdays.

Fishing has changed a great deal on Ozark streams. Time was when all up and down the Meramec, johnboat fishing and pleasure floating were the same, complementing each other like catfish and cornbread. Today the fishing is not as good, and most recreation seekers ply the streams in canoes. The trend is now to get a group together, the bigger the better, rent some canoes and have a party afloat, mostly for one day. Although this is reminiscent of early canoeing on the lower Meramec in the 1920s, there are two major differences. One is that the wooden, canvas-covered craft of the earlier era im-posed a requisite of skill and sobriety upon the participants. Paddlers had to get beyond the bottom-scraping phase allow-able with aluminum or fiberglass hulls; they had to protect the vulnerable skin of canvas from punctures and tearing. A precondition for either rental or ownership demanded some formal instruction. Safety, including the wisdom of never abandoning a swamped canoe even in deep water, came first; nonswimmers were discouraged from participating. The proper strokes of paddling had to be learned in calm water before a person could negotiate gravel-bedded riffles. The second difference is that today on the Meramec most floating is done farther upstream, well beyond the lower valley's deteriorating environment. Headwater natives who enjoy fishing from a johnboat are too often crowded out. Such is the price paid for mass-produced aluminum hulls, convenient rentals and easy transportation.

The most popular portion of the Meramec today is that stretch of it, and of its tributaries the Huzzah and Courtois, saved from damming. We now hoist, or portage, our two canoes over one of the last hog-trough bridges in existence. This one-lane antique of low-water passage links the rugged hills of the Huzzah Wildlife Area with Onondaga Cave State Park, where one of the loveliest commercial caverns anywhere nearly succumbed to permanent inundation.

Some miles downstream we are beckoned to stop and linger along the spectacular curve of the Vilander bluffs. As time allows, I exchange sneakers for hiking boots and clamber up to one of the rocky overlooks two hundred feet above. Sitting down breathlessly on a ledge after the long climb, I grip a gnarled cedar, making sure it is alive and well rooted, trusting its tenacious hold to give me security. From that vantage I witness a succession of weekend canoeists far below, hear their cheerful voices, and catch a wave from my companions lolling on a gravelbar. Beyond this I see a picturesque valley farm dotted with cattle, some heavily wooded hills, and, above it all, a huge blue dome punctuated with turkey vultures lazily circling on set wings. For a brief time my thoughts soar with them; there is a fleeting, frightening urge to try joining them. Closer now, I recheck the cedar's rooted hold, revel in a host of wildflowers and bluestem grass that surround me and are surely invisible from below. Here I am on a miniprairie, a rim-rock glade. It is a world apart, worth all the ticks and

Vilander bluffs, above Meramec State Park.

chiggers I'm collecting because I was so eager to get up here that I forgot to spray myself with insect repellant.

As a last stop before our take-out point, we cool off in the cavernous gape of Green's Cave. Its ninety-foot-high entrance, the largest in Missouri, would have been half covered by the damming a few miles downstream. The cave itself, however, looks rather terminal as it shrinks off to the left, though actually it is not. Without proper caving gear, we dare not explore it beyond visible light, but I know from previous experience that it snakes back under the hills for more than two thousand feet to a mere crawl space. In its twilight zone we can see the ubiquitous work of slobs: broken formations that required many centuries to develop and crude inscriptions made by latter-day Kilroys. This cave and the gravelbar just downstream are quite popular with floaters, and unfortunately they show it. Outside are hacked-upon and initialed trees, as well as trash and used toilet paper waiting to be washed down with the next rise to adjoining Meramec State Park.

Just as we prepare to leave, here comes a sleek fiberglass canoe being propelled upstream through a riffle. It is guided with precision by a man standing amidships and holding nothing but a long pole. With each backward thrust into gravel he not only advances against the current but he also rudders with unerring steadiness. He is an expert devotee of poling and to us stands at the opposite end of the spectrum from those who so commonly desecrate the stream. (I bet he wouldn't insult the scenery with even so much as a tossed-out gum wrapper.) His unusual skill is a tribute to a higher recreation potential.

We take out at Meramec State Park where other canoeists often put in. People float downstream about as far as natural beauty can be perceived and that, of course, is a matter of individual taste. Some people can tolerate more civilized intrusions than others; what is acceptable to one person may be blight to another. For most, however, the Meramec's approach to St. Louis is crowded with too many rows of dilapidated clubhouses, too many gravel diggings, too many furtive dumping places at the mouths of inflowing creeks. Such is the erosion of an urban world that spreads an alluvium of indifference over natural floodplains. It occurs wherever a growing metropolis pushes its way up a lovely stream. The ultimate solution, one forever begging attention but seldom getting it, is a matter of relative values. Must the valley be exploited for commercial interests above all other considerations or should pleasures of the people and quality recreation be granted equal attention? The choice is not really as difficult as it might seem; it is simply a matter of perceiving natural beauty and defending it.

12   Passages Downstream

Although the Meramec has been preserved as one free-flowing entity, it has come to be viewed by the public as separable into two parts. The upper half—including the lovely Huzzah and Courtois—remains a playground for canoeists, johnboaters, gravelbar campers, and, in fact, anyone who admires a natural Ozark stream. After being joined by the Bourbeuse and the Big, the Meramec is looked upon as the lower river, vulnerable to all the kinds of floodplain developments that tend to spread like a blight from metropolitan St. Louis. Half stream, half river, the dividing line is somewhere downstream from Meramec State Park and the site of what was to have been the Corps of Engineers dam. Does this imply that the upper half will always remain a desirable playground? Not necessarily. Does it tell us that the lower half will inexorably continue to deteriorate? We hope not.

Recently, a law applying to the most popular upstream portion, also involving the lower Huzzah and Courtois, was passed by the Missouri legislature to benefit both the local landowners and the canoeing public. In essence, it assures recreation access along most of what would have been drowned by the Meramec reservoir. Choice natural acreages, including the Huzzah Wildlife Area, Onondaga Cave State Park, the spectacular Vilander bluffs, and Green's Cave as part of an expanded Meramec State Park—all are to be retained in state ownership. Lands that were earlier bought by the Corps of Engineers and now returned to private ownership will remain encumbered with scenic easements; that is, the owners may continue using them for agriculture but cannot build new structures. This restriction applies only to about thirty-five miles of the Meramec, leaving the valley farther upstream unprotected. But it does establish a trend, one that promises continuing business for local canoe outfitters and a gradual diminishing of animosities left over from a long-enduring controversy. There will, of course, always be slovenly people attracted to the Meramec who tend to degrade the natural scene. Landowners and canoeists will have to keep reminding themselves that such slobs are the common enemy. In other words, there is a continuing need for mutual trust between local residents and the recreation-seeking public; otherwise a choice Ozark playground may simply be destroyed.

There is one viewpoint that argues that the lower Meramec, the river portion already referred to, should ideally be considered indivisible from the upper stream. All portions could then be managed as one continuous entity. According to nature's scheme this might hold true, but to serve human needs it does not, at least not presently. There is a practical reason for the division, relating to the 1967 study conducted by St. Louis and Jefferson counties, which proposed a National Recreation Area for the lower Meramec. Not only did it focus interest on a sadly neglected resource, but it also became a catalyst for further studies and planning.

In 1969 a brief study by the U.S. Department of the Interior outlined a similar plan to include the entire valley up to Maramec Spring, a channel distance of 168 miles from the Mississippi River. This idea, however, was quickly rejected because it then conflicted directly with Corps of Engineers plans for severing the upper portion with a dam and reservoir. Six years later, however, in 1975, the Department of Interior's Bureau of Outdoor Recreation was granted $50,000 in planning money to revive the idea of a Meramec Recreation Area limited to the lower valley. This proposal, as published a year later with the Missouri Department of Natural Resources, stimulated interest in the original 1967 study and gained wide support because it did not impinge on Corps plans.

Missouri Governor Bond then took a hint from one recommendation of the new study: that all lower Meramec restoration efforts, to have any chance of succeeding, would require close cooperation among municipal, county, state, and private interests. There were too many potential conflicts to do otherwise. Thus, in September 1975, he designated the entire valley below Meramec State Park—a stretch of 108 miles by channel—as the Meramec River Recreation Area (MRRA) and appointed a steering committee to begin planning its development. The coordinating committee was subsequently expanded to involve citizen members from each of the adjoining counties and from every incorporated community in the lower valley.

The MRRA concept, while intended to unite various interests and focus on the neglected resource, did not provide for an authoritarian jurisdictional body; the coordinating committee was granted no legal powers and no means of funding by the state legislature. It was simply to serve the functions of formulating and publicizing a plan where before there had been a void.

The St. Louis County Department of Parks and Recreation, an agency with vested interest in the lower Meramec's recreation potential, became the administrative vehicle for MRRA planning. It served as liaison between the coordinating committee and various agencies, as the agent for MRRA publicity, and as the research arm for the MRRA. Beginning in 1976, the department helped to organize and sponsor the Great Meramec River Raft Float, an annual event of fun, frolic, and media attention for the MRRA. In 1977, the parks department received $2 million from a voter-approved St. Louis County bond issue for purchase and development of park lands within the valley. In 1980, under the leadership of Research Director Ben Knox, the Parks and Recreation department published a detailed planning guide for the MRRA and its coordinating committee.

By then the state was directly involved. Its Department of Natural Resources had just acquired two sizable tracts of land for development into state parks within the lower valley. The Department of Conservation, with funds from its voter-approved ⅛-cent sales tax, was also buying parcels of Meramec land, mostly small access sites for motorboats and canoes.

The designated Meramec River Recreation Area, while separated from the upper stream by jurisdictional and political considerations, serves a worthy purpose. It has already

Each year, the Great Meramec River Raft Float attracts hundreds of canoeists, rafters, and creative floaters for a day of fun sponsored by the St.
Louis County Department of Parks and Recreation.

made people in the St. Lous area more attentive to local recreation needs and potential; it encourages the preservation of
remaining open spaces on the floodplain; it is a stimulus for
cleaning up bankside trash. The concept of the MRRA does
not, however, directly address the issue of periodic flooding.
To many people, and particularly to commercial interests who
cherished ideas of developing the valley, the 1966 Meramec
Basin Plan and its promise of dams was once viewed as the
best solution to controlling floods. But deauthorization of the
dam on the Meramec, and declining support for the others,
has obviously changed all that. Two important questions have
been raised since then. Foremost, if not by dams, how will
the lower valley ever be freed from the damages of rampaging
waters? Secondarily, how can anyone reconcile this problem
with the idealism of the MRRA concept?

Near Winter Park (St. Louis County), this scene may foreshadow development of the Meramec River Recreation Area.

These and related questions became the focus of a detailed
study on reduction of flood damage, published in 1981 by the
Missouri Department of Natural Resources and the now-
defunct Upper Mississippi River Basin Commission. Some
planning critics, recalling forty years of controversy over dams
and where to put them, have argued that various agencies
have just about studied the Meramec to death. This is hardly
possible, however, because any well-subsidized study is begun with a bias of some sort. The very thrust of each study,
therefore, is likely aimed toward preconceived goals. Voluminous data are gathered and analyzed with reference to
specific aims. Projects may be designed for financing by the
taxpaying public. Special interests get involved with their
conflicting viewpoints. Political alliances have to be made if
congressional approval and appropriations are to be won.
While all of this takes place, though, conditions change, new

Valley Park, December 1982.

viewpoints begin to surface like cream on fresh milk, and plans must be reformulated. So it is with any regional planning; so it has been with the Meramec.

The Corps of Engineers has standardized the methods of projecting the scope and frequency of major floods and designing structures to control them. A ten-year flood, as an example, is considered to be of a magnitude to occur on the average of once every ten years; fifty-year and hundred-year floods are predicted accordingly. Based on these odds, a series of dams may thus be designed to control a hundred-year crest and a system of agricultural levees to keep a fifty-year flood from inundating valley farmland. Size limits of the project structures are determined by various economic considerations that, in the case of dams, must include the cost of relocation for homes, highways, utilities, and other developments in the way. Yet none of this promises any guarantee against floods that just happen to exceed design limitations.

The Bourbeuse crest of December 1982, the greatest flood crest in its recorded history, was estimated to be in the range of a five-hundred year occurrence. The reservoir that had been proposed for this tributary could not have held back the floodwaters even if it had already been in place at full, or flood, pool. This point is pertinent simply because floods have a nasty way of recurring over rather short intervals. And such recurrences are not mere coincidence; the inherent nature of midwestern climate brings definite cycles of very wet and then very droughty years. The wettest years tend to leave the ground deeply saturated for months at a time. Repeated downpours then result in accelerated runoff and flood-control reservoirs may remain full, or nearly full, until the next deluge. There is no way for the Corps of Engineers to predict such trends, in spite of their expertise. These matters and others were considered in the flood damage reduction study of 1981, which, indirectly, might be said to have predicted the great flooding of the Meramec basin in 1982, prior to scheduled completion of any of the Corps dams—even the first on the Meramec. And the question of just how much difference a series of dams would have made is debatable. One thing is certain: none could have prevented the flood by itself.

Fittingly entitled *Out of Harm's Way*, the 1981 study was biased toward the premise that nature has created floodplains for flooding and that dams, levees, and other large and costly structures cannot protect against all floods. It emphasized that their construction often imposes unwarranted damage upon the natural environment and that they have grown too expensive for federal budgeting that is grossly overextended by deficit spending. Furthermore, the federally subsidized National Flood Insurance Program, instigated in 1967 to reimburse property owners for water damages, and the flood emergency services for personal hardship cases are becoming undue burdens to American taxpayers. Many highlanders have lost sympathy for people who insist on residing within floodways and are then permitted to buy the subsidized flood insurance for doing so or must be granted disaster aid if they have no such coverage. The high price of living on flood-prone land is sadly illustrated by the case of Times Beach on the lower Meramec—regardless of the former town's misfortunes with dioxin.

Times Beach acquired its name from a now-defunct St. Louis newspaper, the *Times*, which sold cottage lots there in the 1920s. An individual buying two lots, each only twenty feet wide, could acquire title to a third one for the mere purchase price of a newspaper subscription; this provided minimal space for the proud riverside landowner to build a summer cottage. From cottage colony begun as a promotional scheme, Times Beach eventually grew into a permanent settlement. By 1973, when the community first applied for National Flood Insurance privileges, it was 90 percent residential and more than 90 percent on the floodplain; obviously, it qualified. But in 1981, because its citizens narrowly voted down a federal requirement that the town implement a plan for moving to higher ground—presumably on hilly land to be purchased across the channel—they lost all privileges of flood insurance. The town's official response was that the residents could not afford to move and were not about to plan or legislate themselves out of existence.

Times Beach had already suffered partial flooding on numerous occasions and total inundation in 1945 and 1957. But the highest water came on 6 December 1982, when the local Meramec gage read nearly twenty-one feet above flood stage. Oddly enough, although the river was slightly higher than the previous high in 1915, years before the town existed, it moved less water. The 1915 flood was estimated to have carried 175,000 cubic feet of water per second of flow, but the 1982 crest indicated only 145,000 cubic feet per second. The apparent reason is a man-made obstruction in the natural floodway. The Interstate 44 right-of-way, elevated across the valley, partially blocked the flood by funneling all water through a solitary gap beneath the Meramec bridge. This action created a backpressure of surging water right into Times Beach. The highway proved to be, in effect, a partial levee just down-

Times Beach, December 1982.

stream from the beleaguered town. The demise of Times Beach, however, was caused neither by flooding nor by the problems of its citizens in getting flood insurance protection. Dioxin killed Times Beach.

A residual product from various synthetic poisons, dioxin is highly damaging to many functions of the human body, apparently even in very small concentrations of a few parts per billion. The least of its symptoms are exhibited on the skin as various dermatological problems; among its worst effects are hormonal imbalances, loss of immunological response to certain infections, neuropsychiatric reactions, and possible genetic defects in unborn children. The dioxin at Times Beach was deposited by a hauler of waste materials who had it transported from a former chemical plant at Verona, Missouri. Instead of disposing it properly as a potentially hazardous substance, he mixed it with oil, which he contracted to spray in horsebarns and on roads where dust was a nuisance, including the streets of Times Beach. Although the contaminated oil was sprayed in the 1970s, the dioxin was not discovered until after the flood of 1982, and only because contract records of the hauler, Russell M. Bliss, indicated he had done so. Because dioxin is soluble only in a lipid medium—oil, for example—and therefore not readily mixed with water, it is highly unlikely that more than a very little of it was spread by the flood. It remained in the streets of Times Beach. Its widely publicized presence in Times Beach, however, precipitated the ultimate buy-out of the town at taxpayer expense; it also relieved its departing citizens of any further flood damages. Perhaps in fitting irony, the town born by a newspaper may have been killed as much by media attention as by dioxin. We know that the chemical is dangerous, but we do not know to what extent. In an earlier era, the people of Times Beach would have likely stayed on—to an unknown future, to be sure. But media coverage of hazardous wastes has stirred nearly hysterical responses among many people, although probably with good reason. Political expediency, especially in response to charges made in 1982 against the federal Environmental Protection Agency for failure to act efficiently in cases of hazardous waste removal from known contaminated sites, demanded that the Reagan administration step in quickly. The residents of Times Beach have been moved, but the dioxin issue per se remains unsettled.

So, too, does flood control. Currently, the most economical and environmentally acceptable solution to Meramec flooding is being considered in terms of yielding the floodplain to its natural function. This solution calls for no more development where flooding is most likely to occur. Although it has always been easier and cheaper to build on low, rock-free alluvial ground, it has also been more risky, as flood records have so often proved. Further damages could be reduced by establishing floodway zoning to guide future development onto higher ground. New residences and other building would not be permitted on the most vulnerable areas. Those established there might then be removed whenever it becomes economically feasible.

According to this scheme of regional management, additional measures to lessen flood damages would be required. Among these might be the paving of municipal areas with water-absorbant materials to retard runoff, aligning elevated highways and other landfills so as not to impede the movement of floodwaters, offering tax inducements to use low areas for agriculture and recreation, and tightening restrictions for participation in the National Flood Insurance Program. No single measure could promise protection for the entire valley any more than levees or upstream dams. All together, however, they would surely prove that costly engineering works are not the only means for dealing with nature's exasperating ways.

There is one possible exception to the nonstructural scheme for solving Meramec flood problems. It applies to those areas downstream from the town of Valley Park that are prone to backwater inundation from the Mississippi River. Flood-control structures have long been an established fact along the Mississippi. They exist in the form of high levees on both sides of the channel that constrict its overflow and therefore elevate its major flood crests. Such moving, surging water has to go somewhere, and there is no way to keep it from causing backwater flooding along the lower Meramec, particularly around the towns of Arnold, Fenton, and Valley Park. It is often argued that for a short distance above its mouth, the Meramec might justifiably merit levee protection. As of this writing, the Corps of Engineers has been authorized to spend $20 million on flood protection along the lower valley; the only stipulation is that no dams are to be built. Levees are being considered, but an important point to consider is the price tag. When built for agricultural protection, they are normally designed to fifty-year flood specifications. On the lower Meramec they might need to be much higher. The

An elk strides stoically at Lone Elk County Park, between Valley Park and
   Times Beach.

question is whether $20 million would be enough for such
levees (and, if not, would more be justified).

On the other hand, the nonstructural approach is in beautiful accord with the Meramec River recreation concept. It im-
plies reserving the most flood-prone areas for recreation,
natural areas, and agriculture. Whatever water damages occur in such places are then kept to a minimum, barely visible
after a normal growing season. Nature heals quickly with
greenery—no risks, no salvage costs, no excessive burdens to
the taxpayers. The only displacements are a gravelbar here, a
mud bank there, some toppled trees skirting the channel.

One of the most vulnerable areas on the Meramec had
been the community of Times Beach. The tragedy of its dioxin problem generated nationwide publicity, but it also had
suffered many floods. When the last traces of poison have disappeared, likely buried under alluvium brought down from

upstream, the place will probably become a natural area for enjoyment of the people. It will then be a symbol of redemption for human errors. By that time the downstream Meramec might better be understood, not feared and denigrated. People might then appreciate the MRRA concept and the natural floodplain. They might also look way upstream and view the whole basin as one living entity to serve the needs of all admirers.

Selected References

Branson, E. B. *Geology of Missouri*. Columbia: University of Missouri Press, 1944.

Bretz, J. Harlen. *Caves of Missouri*. Rolla: Missouri Geological Survey and Water Resources, 1956.

Bretz, J. Harlen. *Geomorphic History of the Ozarks of Missouri*. Rolla: Missouri Geological Survey and Water Resources, 1965.

Buchanan, Alan C. *Mussels of the Meramec River Basin*. Jefferson City: Missouri Department of Conservation, 1980.

Chapman, Carl H. *The Archaeology of Missouri*. 2 vols. Columbia: University of Missouri Press, 1975 and 1980.

Eschbach, Walter L. *A Proposal for a National Recreation Area on the Lower Meramec River*. Joint Study by Jefferson County Planning and Zoning Commission and St. Louis County Planning Commission, 1967.

Gaffney, Richard M. *Out of Harm's Way—Lower Meramec Valley Flood Damage Reduction Study*. Jefferson City: Missouri Department of Natural Resources, 1981.

Hawksley, Oz. *Missouri Ozark Waterways*. Jefferson City: Missouri Department of Conservation, 1968.

Ingenthron, Elmo. *Indians of the Ozark Plateau*. Point Lookout, Mo.: School of the Ozarks Press, 1970.

Knox, Ben. *Lower Meramec River Management Study*. Clayton, Mo.: Meramec River Recreation Area Coordinating Committee and St. Louis County Department of Parks and Recreation, 1980.

LaVal, Richard K., et al. *An Evaluation of the Status of Myotene Bats in the Proposed Meramec Park Lake and Union Lake Project Areas*. Columbia: School of Forestry, Fisheries, and Wildlife, University of Missouri, for the U.S. Army Corps of Engineers, 1980.

Marshall, Richard A. *Prehistoric Indians at Maramec Spring Park*. New York: Lucy Wortham James Foundation, 1966.

Mehl, M. G. *Missouri's Ice Age Mammals*. Rolla: Missouri Geological Survey and Water Resources, 1962.

Morrison, John A. *As the River Flows*. Anderson, Ind.: Anderson College Press, 1962.

Norris, James D. *Frontier Iron—The Maramec Iron Works 1826–1876*. Madison: The State Historical Society of Wisconsin, 1964.

137

Pflieger, William L. *The Fishes of Missouri*. Jefferson City: Missouri Department of Conservation, 1975.

Rafferty, Milton D. *The Ozarks Land and Life*. Norman: University of Oklahoma Press, 1962.

Sauer, Carl O. *The Geography of the Ozark Highland*. Chicago: University of Chicago Press, 1920.

Schwartz, Charles W. and Elizabeth R. Schwartz. *The Wild Mammals of Missouri*. Rev. ed. Columbia: University of Missouri Press and Missouri Department of Conservation, 1981.

Sugerman, Jerry M. *Meramec Heritage Riverway Plan*. Sullivan, Mo.: Meramec Heritage Association, 1977.

Ulman, E. L., R. R. Boyce, and D. J. Volk. *The Meramec Basin, Water and Economic Development*. St. Louis: Meramec Basin Corporation and Washington University, 1962.

Unklesbay, A. G. *The Common Fossils of Missouri*. Columbia: University of Missouri Press, 1956.

U.S. Army Corps of Engineers. *Meramec River Comprehensive Basin Plan*. St. Louis: Corps of Engineers, St. Louis District, 1964.

U.S. Army Corps of Engineers. *Meramec Park Lake Environmental Statement*. St. Louis: Corps of Engineers, St. Louis District, 1973.

U.S. Army Corps of Engineers. *Union Lake, Bourbeuse River, Environmental Statement*. St. Louis: Corps of Engineers, St. Louis District, 1974.

Vineyard, Jerry D. and Gerald L. Feder. *Springs of Missouri*. Rolla: Missouri Geological Survey and Water Resources, 1974.

Weaver, Dwight H. and Paul A. Johnson. *Missouri: The Cave State*. Jefferson City: Discovery Enterprises, 1980.

Willoughby, Harvey. *Report to St. Louis District, Corps of Engineers, on the Effects of the Authorized Meramec Park Lake, Missouri, on Fish and Wildlife*. Kansas City: U.S. Department of the Interior, Fish and Wildlife Service, 1976.

Willoughby, Harvey. *Report to St. Louis District, Corps of Engineers, on the Effects of the Authorized Union Lake, Missouri, on Fish and Wildlife Resources*. Kansas City: U.S. Department of the Interior, Fish and Wildlife Service, 1976.